Yosemite Trails

Yosemite Trails

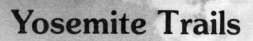

Western Trails Publications

Lew & Ginny Clark

TUOLUMNE MEADOWS   Gerald Born, NPS

© Lewis W. Clark & Virginia D. Clark, 1976
Revised edition, 1979, 1983
All rights reserved
Library of Congress Catalogue Card Number 76-19361
ISBN 0-931532-01-9

Western Trails Publications
P.O. Box 1697
San Luis Obispo, CA 93406

4

MOUNTAIN BREEZE

I wish I were a mountain breeze
      That wanders on o'er hill and dale
      Sighing softly through stalwart trees
      And caressing flowers in mountain vale.

I'd wander up the canyon walls
      Where cliff swallows dart and sway,
      Then pause to listen in wooded halls
      Where warblers sing and chickarees play.

I'd drift along the river's breast
      Capturing the fragrance of azalia bowers
      And drifting on o'er waterfall's crest
      Gather mists for summer showers.

Then, once again I'd sweep the crests
      Along skyline's glacial cirques, and
      There in quiet contentment rest
      In wonderment at our Creator's works.

—Lewis W. Clark
1904—1979

CONTENTS

Yosemite Wilderness

Up and beyond the canyon rims of Yosemite Valley lies a vast wilderness area covering some 1200 square miles of rugged, undeveloped backcountry. Much of it stands well above 8000 feet elevation and contains hundreds of miles of lakeshore and streams.

It is made up of three main watersheds: the Tuolumne River and its tributaries that drain most of what is called Yosemite's North Country; the South Fork of the Merced that drains the broad, wooded basins lying along the south boundary of the Park; and the main Merced River that draws upon the Tenaya, Merced, and Illilouette canyons for its waters that flow into Yosemite Valley down plunging cascades and from hanging valleys in sheer, free-falling waterfalls. The crests of mountain ranges marking these watershed boundaries stand well above the 10,000 feet level while basins between them contain more than 450 lakes and some 100 named streams to lure the climber, fisherman and backpacker who just came to look.

Yosemite is the northern climax of the immense cordillera—the Sierra Nevada. It is a part of the longest and most extensively trailed range in the United States. Except for occasional summer afternoon showers it has some two to three months of ideal camping weather between June and October.

Its extensive and varied tree cover is of an "open-forest" character that invites entry and permits long stretches of cross-country travel. The lower forest is made up of oaks, pines and conifers of unusual size. Above this lies the red-fir forest, one of the largest virgin stands of its kind. Backcountry hikers soon move up beyond this great forest to experience the wonderland that has become identified as "The High Sierra." Up to treeline the region is primarily forested by lodgepole pine interspersed with the lovely mountain hemlock, western white pine, and western juniper.

On the shoulders of the higher, glacier-worn ridges is nature's vanguard troops of whitebark pine challenging the barrenness of her alpine slopes. They lie like crouching invaders in the shelter of huge granite ledges awaiting the opportunity to implant one more of their small force above them. Their extended arms, though sheered by freezing, sleet-laden winds, turn to creeping along in sheltered nooks for hundreds of years in defiance of their adversaries.

Above here the alpine setting becomes more definite. Most life is limited to tundra-like grasses, dwarf red and white heather nestled against giant boulders, sky-blue polemonium scattered among rocks and crags, and the miniature alpine willow.

Near the talus slopes the cony is busy cutting his hay crop for the coming winter. The rosy finch gathers frozen insects from nearby snow fields and builds his nest in rocky nitches on a sheer cliff high above the ice fields. In splendid reward for his arduous labor, our hay-gathering mountaineer is serenaded by Rosy's lovely song establishing his territorial claims and ardor to his modest mate nearby. As evening draws near ...

> The twinkling stars of Sierra nights
>> Look down on the mountains wrapped in snow
>> A chorus of winds along the lofty heights
>> Mingles with the roar of streams below
>
> Home of the rosy finch, polemonium, and cony
>> And alpine willow and cassiope dwell;
>> In meadows, chimneys, and landslides stony
>> The wildfolk of nature live in its spell.
>
> Land of antiquity! Going back in time
>> For its glacial crags and cirques;
>> Engaging the elements of every clime
>> To carry on its tremendous works.
>
> With summer's rain and winter's snow
>> The quarrying glaciers grind their flour;
>> And the rivulets and streams in canyons below
>> Carry the unending toil of creation's hour.

— LWC

The Landscape

The story of Yosemite's High Sierra is a story of the past. To pause and meditate on a skyline crest brings a deep sense of mystery that prevails over the entire region. Here the secrets of the past are exposed to view in the empty graves of ancient cirques and time is measured in glacial epochs; we are looking upon a land still in its infancy in the evolution of our mountains.

From the level floors of deep canyons to the last skyline glacial cirque, one is ever aware of the unseen presence of momentous forces of nature and time that once pervaded this entire region.

The vast expanse of the wilderness area of Yosemite presents, with its ever-changing panorama, certain consistent patterns of geological formations such as: the sheer U-shaped canyons; the giant stairstep floors of deep valleys giving rise to roaring cascades and plunging waterfalls; level valley floors supporting flat meadows and tall trees testifying to the deep, sediment-filled basins beneath them; the glacial polished walls and turns of bare, granitoid canyons; and along near the skyline ridges, glacial cirques and ponds, graveyards of glaciers long gone.

There are some 60 glaciers still active in the entire Sierra Nevada block. Those most active in the Yosemite region are found on Lyell, McClure, Dana, Conness peaks, and the Matterhorn Crest. They are well above the 11,000 foot elevation and are remnants of what is referred to as the Little Ice Age of comparatively recent geological times. In the long story of mountain building, they are relatively young, having their beginnings later than 2000 B.C.

The origin and survival of these glaciers has been due to certain favorable conditions. All are found in deep, cirque-like pockets on north and northeast sides of peaks in which snow has been trapped by the prevailing westerly and south-westerly winds; and all are hugged close to sheer cliffs which shade them much of the day, even during the summer months. Such sun as they are exposed to reaches them in long, slanting rays devoid of most of their melting powers.

The largest of Yosemite's ancient glaciers was in the Tuolumne Canyon and its many laterals. Some 60 miles in length, it lay like a great mantle up to 2000 feet thick over much of a great basin some 500 miles square. As it moved down into and through the Tuolumne River Canyon it ranged up to 5000 feet in thickness.

In the earlier Ice Ages of Yosemite it is estimated that ice in the upper part of Yosemite Valley reached a thickness of 3000 feet. However, not all of Yosemite's High Sierra was covered by glaciers. Many of the extreme summits of ridges and peaks were kept clear of accumulating snows by strong prevailing winds and glaciers never had a chance to form. As the massive rivers of ice moved along they were bypassed and left standing like stark, granite islands in a vast sea of flowing, glittering ice.

Those interested in the materials and evidences of glacial action will find much to satisfy them in the Merced, Tenaya, and Tuolumne canyons. Lateral moraines are found paralleling both the north and south rims of Little Yosemite. Weather pits are evident on most of the domes and glacial polish, chattermarks, and grooves can be seen between the Twin Bridges crossing of the Merced River and the lower end of Merced Lake. Boulder gardens or erratics are well represented in the area along the High Trail canyon rim overlooking Lost Valley and Twin Bridges. In the upper Lyell Fork of the Tuolumne, especially after heavy rains, one can see glacial flour turning the waters milky-white flowing down from Lyell Glacier. In basins above the canyons, flower decked meadows now fill ancient glacial tarns. Wherever we look and whenever we listen, we see and hear the ever-expanding views and sounds of the tremendous forces of nature that wrought this wonderland of the Yosemite High Sierra.

As the glaciers moved down the present Tenaya and Merced canyons they converged between Half Dome and Glacier Point. Their extensive activity had loosened great quantities of rock material which was carried along with it. Some of this was rolled out along the sides of canyons as *lateral moraines* and some was pushed ahead of the main block of ice and piled up into a broad *dike* or *terminal moraine* below El Capitan.

When the glacial era subsided this great dike acted as a dam across the lower end of Yosemite Valley. The melting ice and snows then filled the basin to form ancient Lake Yosemite. This lake gradually disappeared as silt, sand and rock material were washed and rolled down from the higher slopes. In some sections of the valley this deposit was more than 1000 feet deep, accounting for its level, deeply wooded character today.

In the higher areas of the Park the glacial valleys are less advanced in their stage of development and are mostly rounded and U-shaped at the bottom with evidences of *glacial polish* shining in the sunlight. Yosemite's glaciers, even though small, are true glaciers and provide excellent examples of what ancient predecessors did in the formation of the Sierra.

LATERAL MORAINES AT GREEN CREEK AND ROBINSON CREEK

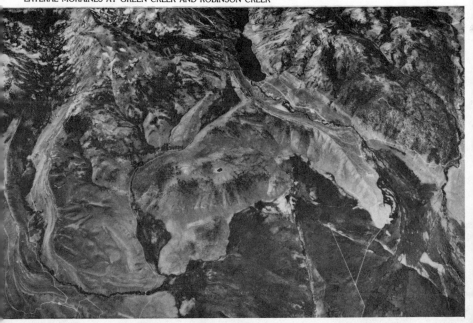

FOR PAGE 143

Yosemite ... "was enlivened and made glorious with rejoicing streams that come chanting in chorus over the cliffs and through side canyons in falls of every conceivable form, to join the river in tranquil, shining beauty."
— John Muir

The number and type of waterfalls and cascades along the Merced and Tuolumne rivers are a living testimony of the results of the ancient glacial activity. *Hanging valleys* and *stairstep canyons* provide a grand display in early season.

Although the highest falls are located in the Yosemite Valley canyon, and the most spectacular ones on the Tuolumne River around Glen Aulin, the descent of all other backcountry streams from high, snow-filled basins to lower main canyons and lakes provides hundreds of smaller falls and cascades, each with its own distinctive contribution.

The glacial action story goes on and on. The only thing constant in the Sierra is the process of change as "the everlasting hills" are being slowly eroded to join the sediments of ancient Sierra landscapes in the lower valleys.

NPS PHOTO

ILLILOUETTE FALL   WHITE CASCADES

Yosemite Fall (upper is 1,430′, lower is 320′) is seen from several places along the south canyon rim. Views from Glacier Point give the finest perspective as to the fall's real size and beauty.

No matter what season—the full burst of spring runoff or the lean autumn dribble, the magnificence is uncomparable. As the falls decline in volume the marked rocks show the power that was. In winter various water and ice conditions present fascinating variations as great sheets of ice are frozen to the cliffs, subsequently to fall thundering to the valley below.

Bridalveil Fall (620′) dominates the lower end of the valley. Its real beauty is best appreciated near its base where the drifting spray shows the appropriateness of its name. From the Old Stage Road well up on the north side of the canyon wall at sundown you can see the up-canyon winds separate the falls into great clouds of rainbow spray. Truly it is one of the most beautiful sights of all Yosemite. Occasionally the rainbow-hued spray is picked up and the whole stream is blown back over the top, to fall again as spray.

Other falls in the lower part of the Valley that are usually dried up by early midsummer are:

Silver Strand Falls (1170′) can be seen near the west end of the Valley on the south side. For many years they were known as *Widows Tears* due to the short duration of their display.

Ribbon Fall (1612′) once known as *Virgins Tears* is the highest single fall of Yosemite. It can be seen from the north side opposite Bridalveil Fall.

Sentinel Falls (2000′) plunges over the south rim in a chain ending in a 500′ drop. This descending cascade is seen from the north side near Three Brothers and from the southwest of the Four-Mile Trail parking area.

Staircase Falls (1300′) is best seen from the Camp Curry Area. It is made up of many short falls draining out of Staircase Creek Canyon to the right of Glacier Point.

Illilouette Fall (370′) can be seen from the trail between Happy Isles and Vernal Fall Bridge, and from several points between the Illilouette Creek Bridge and Glacier Point.

HIGH SIERRA LOOP TRAIL

SIERRA POINT	0.7
VERNAL FALL BRIDGE	0.8
TOP OF VERNAL FALL	1.5
TOP OF NEVADA FALL	3.4
GLACIER POINT	8.2
HALF DOME	8.2
CLOUDS REST	10.5
MERCED LAKE	13.1
TENAYA LAKE	16.4
TUOLUMNE MEADOWS	27.3
MOUNT WHITNEY — (JOHN MUIR TRAIL)	211.0

Here at Happy Isles Trailhead the song of birds, the noisy, tumbling waters, and being surrounded by three thousand foot canyon walls, is a most joyous beginning for backcountry trips.

Yosemite Trail System

The beginning of Yosemite's trail system goes back to the primitive Miwok tribes such as the Ah-wa-niches who followed the deer from the low, sheltered winter valleys into the high mountain canyons and meadows as spring edged into summer and alpine meadows became brief pasture lands for Nature's families.

Following the Indians came the stockmen, miners, and timber cruisers seeking the lush meadows, mineral treasure and timber for homes and commerce. Then, as such pioneer mountaineers as LeConte and Muir gave direction and meaning to the mysteries of this land the passing riches of commerce were replaced by an appreciation of the real wealth of the scenic wonders of *The Incomparable Yosemite*.

More and more trails penetrated the unknown Sierra wilderness. They extended beyond the scattered paths of migrating deer and eager pioneers. Placed first under the Army cavalry's protection, then under state and federal foresters and later, under the National Park Service, the trail system has expanded to some 700 miles. Each season the Engineering and Patrol Ranger departments make improvements on both the trails and their extensive system of signs covering the important trail heads, junctions and special features. The Forest Service, which manages the National Forest Wilderness Areas surrounding Yosemite, has developed campgrounds and trails which provide a more accessible entry into what was once a remote, seldom visited region.

The accuracy of mileage was determined by making metered wheel measurements on foot. Patrol Rangers and the Engineering Departments have worked together to verify their information and to keep it current. This data, along with extensive explorations by the writers between Yosemite, Kern River-Sequoia country and adjacent wilderness areas has provided a reasonably accurate base of information for this guide. Maps are made consistent with the USGS topo maps. Trail Profiles indicate the general terrain between camping sites, trail junctions, and important physical features.

LEGEND

RANGER STATION	
CAMPGROUND	
WC: WALK-IN CAMPGROUND	

MAIN TRAIL

ALTERNATE ROUTE

CROSS COUNTRY

JOHN MUIR TRAIL

PACIFIC CREST TRAIL

5.8 Mileages Between Points

Contour Lines Indicating Change in Elevation 80 FEET

SCALE

UNLESS OTHERWISE INDICATED:
Top of all maps is NORTH
Contour interval is 80 feet
Scale: 1 inch=one mile
Trail routes & Mileages: Based upon Park Engineer's data and current trail reports of Park Rangers.

PARK BOUNDARY

ROAD (SURFACED)

ROAD (UNSURFACED)

HIGH SIERRA CAMP

SADDLE HORSES AVAILABLE

P Backcountry Parking

FISH USUALLY TAKEN:
R: Rainbow, EB: Eastern Brook
G: Golden, B: Brown

"Duc"

Early Day "Blaze"

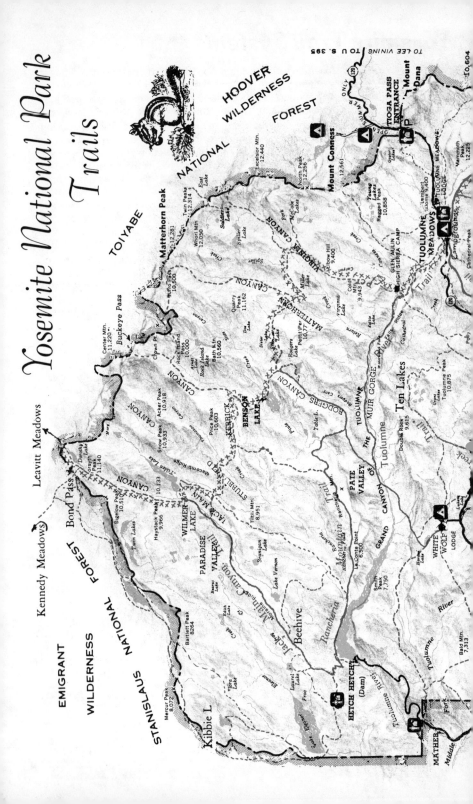

Yosemite National Park
Trails

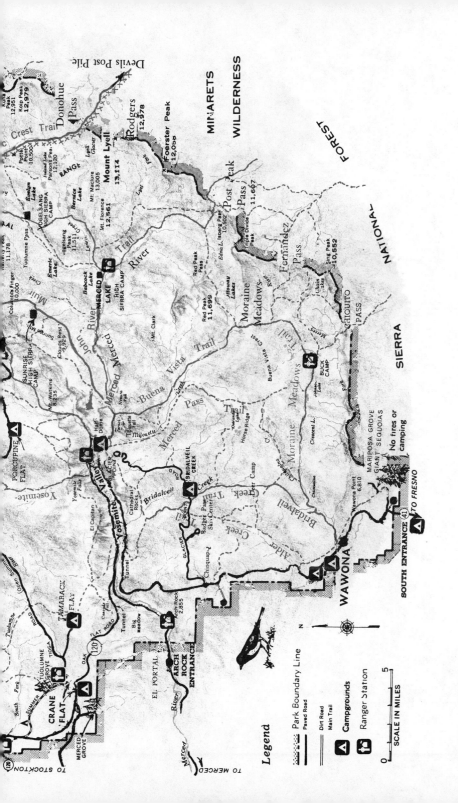

Yosemite Valley

New arrivals at National Parks seek out the Visitor Center for information on what their special features are. Actually, the whole of Yosemite Valley is a "visitor center" for the 1200 square miles of the Yosemite's backcountry. Here, between El Capitan, Mirror Lake, and Nevada Fall, is found the complete environmental story of the Sierra.

Upon entering the Valley, plan to park your car. Free shuttle buses will transport you close to trailheads at Happy Isles, Mirror Lake, or Yosemite Falls. Buses run frequently to all facilities including the campgrounds, Village Mall, Awahnee Hotel, Yosemite Lodge, and Visitor Center.

The Visitor Center displays natural, geological, and historical exhibits. Ranger Naturalists are on duty to answer questions, and to conduct walks and evening programs. On sale are books, pamphlets, and maps. Behind the Center is the Indian Village—a visit to the past life of the Miwok Indians.

If you like company, take one of the daily conducted tours by the Ranger Naturalist. If you prefer solitude or a non-scheduled walk, take your lunch and camera, board a bus to a trailhead, and wander along one of the many trails paralleling the roads and canyon walls on both sides of the Merced River.

Bring your bikes—grown-ups and kids—and enjoy many happy hours traveling along the numerous Valley floor trails. For those without bikes, they can be rented at Curry Village where maps of specific trails can be secured.

Horseback rides from one hour to a full day are available. There are escorted trips for children as well as adults along the Valley floor. Some half-day and all-day trips are made to Half Dome, Clouds Rest, and Nevada Falls. Check at the stables for rates and time of the various trips.

Yosemite Valley Trailhead

MERCED RIVER
JOHN
OLD FOOT TRAIL 1.0 ONLY
NEVADA FALL 594' DROP
STREAMBED
BRIDGE
PICNIC AREA
5,900 .2
STARR KING CR.
MUIR
GLACIER
MERCED PASS TRAIL

DIAMOND CASCADE
SILVER APRON
BRIDGE
CLARK POINT 5,480
.4
6,600

EMERALD POOL
STAIRS
Spring
TRAIL
POINT

VERNAL FALL 317' DROP
MIST TRAIL
.5
.3
TRAIL
TRAIL
1.0

RIVER
TRAIL
.5

SIERRA POINT 5,450
BRIDGE
PANORAMA CLIFF 6,650
ILLILOUETTE FALL 370' DROP
BRIDGE 5,850
1.7
2.

MERCED RIVER
TRAIL ONLY 1.2

SPRING
JOHN
ILLILOUETTE CREEK
.8

STABLES
PARKING AREA
HAPPY ISLES 4,034
HORSE
6,400

N
LOOKOUT
1.4

OVERHANGING ROCK
GLACIER POINT 7,214'
T

This beautiful canyon is the most popular of any region in the Park for easy, short hikes. Here, within the space of a few miles, is concentrated nearly all the things people seek in the mountains. Tremendous heights of sheer granite walls, views into deep gorges filled with white cascades and magnificent waterfalls are all made accessible by wide, well-graded trails.

Although all trails in this Giant Stairway Canyon are safe they must be followed with care. Do not short-cut or venture out on ledges for better views as this is a hazardous region. Hikers should allow the better part of a day to make a round trip to the crest of Nevada Fall. Under NO conditions go out into flowing waters or on to the slick polished rocks. Those with stock must use the trail on the southeast side of the river between Happy Isles and the junction above the bridge.

The Sierra Point trail is not recommended for general use because it is quite steep, unmaintained and slightly hazardous. Beyond this junction is the short up-hill walk to the Vernal Fall Bridge. Here is one of the finest views of the Fall with the foaming, tumbling waters plunging down beneath you. About .2 mile after crossing to the east side of the river, the trail divides.

It is a long, three and a half miles to the top of Nevada Fall. Those with heavy packs will do well to stick to the main trail where the higher route gives broader views of the canyon and the long switchbacks require less effort than the steep, and at places very wet, Mist Trail below Vernal Fall, or the rough foot trail between Vernal and Nevada falls.

The Mist Trail is a foot trail only. The spray from Vernal creates a green carpet of moss and ferns. The trail is safe with steep, stone-steps which are solid, although somewhat slippery at times from the moisture. It is strenuous to climb up these talus boulders as the cool drenching spray soaks to the skin. Near the top the precipitous sections have pipe railings. The thunderous tumult of the falls with its tumbling force is tremendous.

A much drier, longer, and easier trip to the top of Vernal Fall can be made by the switchbacks of the well-graded John Muir Trail along the south canyon wall. The views from this canyon along the trail are most impressive.

Beyond Vernal are the Emerald Pool, Spray Apron, and Diamond Cascade where the whole river rushes over smooth rocks and develops speed before the final plunge over the crest.

A hiker's trail crosses the river (by bridge) to the north side of the stream. It ascends to the head of the canyon via steep, rough switchbacks that follow up the old course of the Merced River before great rock slides diverted the waters to its present free-leaping Nevada Fall. Along the trail are found huge Douglas Firs which favor this moist, cool canyon. There are several unusual viewpoints close to the roaring cascades.

NPS PHOTO

SOUTH VALLEY RIM TRAILS

The most popular view of Yosemite Valley and the surrounding high country is from Glacier Point. From there, three thousand feet below, is seen the Merced River meandering through meadows and scattered groves of pines and firs. The spectacular, panoramic view of the vast backcountry with its many sheer granite walls, domes, and peaks, extend to the far-flung boundaries of the Park.

At Happy Isles below, is the confluence of Tenaya Creek and the Merced River. It was here the ancient glaciers met to combine their forces to carve out the magnificent valley. The Tenaya Canyon scene includes the imposing Half Dome and Clouds Rest, several great domes, and views up to Tenaya Peak and Mt. Hoffman.

To the east are the entire river basins of the Merced and Illilouette. It is an impressive panorama of the Great Stairway Canyon with Vernal and Nevada Falls, Little Yosemite, up the Merced Canyon to the Sierra crest peaks of Mts. Lyell, McClure and Florence. To the right is Mt. Starr King and the Clark Range. Another equally expansive view of the Clark Range is from Washburn Point—a short distance on the road south of Glacier Point.

NPS PHOTO

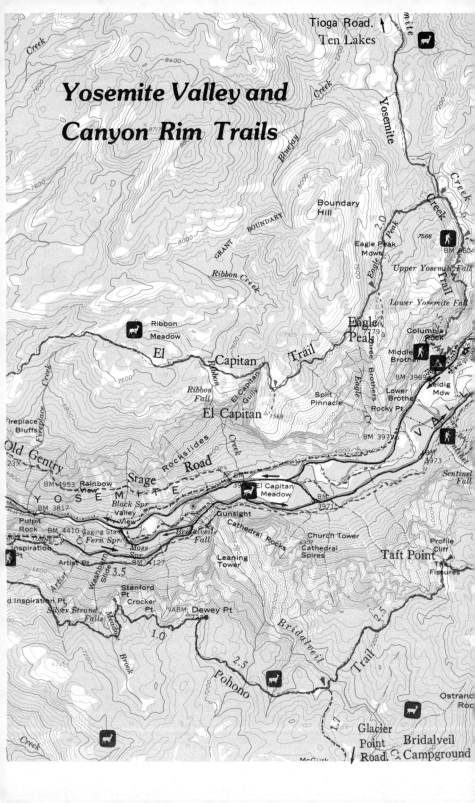

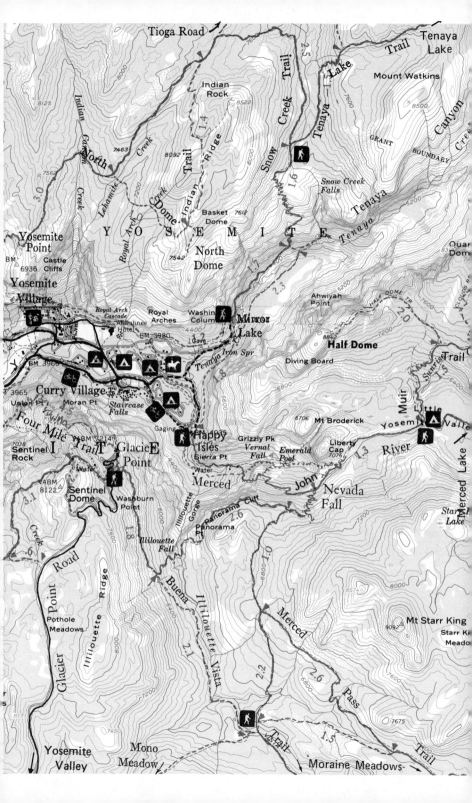

SIERRA SETTING   EUGENE ROSE

SOUTH VALLEY RIM TRAILS

Both Glacier Point and Mono Meadows are an ideal trailhead to start for country to the south and east. See trails and maps pages 48 - 55. Several South Valley Rim Trails start here also. Public transportation is available to Glacier Point and to the Mariposa Grove.

GLACIER POINT TRAIL (Total 8.3 miles; an all day trip) Starting at Happy Isles on the Valley floor, the trail goes up to Glacier Point via Nevada Fall, Panorama Cliffs, and Illilouette Creek (see map page 22). The trip back can be made by the Four-Mile Trail as it is too long to return via the Pohono Trail the same day.

THE FOUR-MILE TRAIL descends the canyon wall by a series of well-graded switchbacks 1.8 miles to Union Point where broad views up and down the Valley delight the photographer. From here on down the trail follows along the foot of the sheer face of Sentinel Rock. (Telephones and comfort stations are at Glacier Point.) Positively no short cutting on these switchbacks as it is very dangerous

Sentinel Dome can be reached by the Pohono Trail or by the trail from the Glacier Point Road. From its summit is one of the very finest views. Here, one can see west into the hazy reaches of the San Joaquin Valley, north across the Yosemite Valley gorge to the headwaters of Yosemite Creek, east to the great Sierra crest, and south up the Illilouette Basin to the Triple Divide country along the Park's south boundary. The dramatic, lone Jeffrey pine on the summit is probably one of the most photographed pines in the world.

Another fine view of the Valley is from Taft Point. From the Glacier Point Road it is an easy trail that contours through beautiful wooded slopes to the rim of Yosemite Valley.

THE POHONO TRAIL   (See map page 26). To get the most out of this trip start at Glacier Point. The trail runs through a secluded, primitive area of fairly uniform elevation as far west as Dewey Point. This country provides many breathtaking views of Yosemite Valley from Crocker, Stanford, Dewey, and Old Inspiration points. Camping is now permitted on the Pohono Trail between the Bridalveil Creek bridge and Fort Monroe. Bridalveil Creek Campground is some 2.8 miles south via the Alder Creek Trail. Check with the Ranger for other camping areas as you get your required Wilderness Permit.

This trail is especially enjoyable in the spring with a profusion of flowers, open meadows, alternating with dense forest, and active wildlife—deer, bear and a host of birds of many varieties.

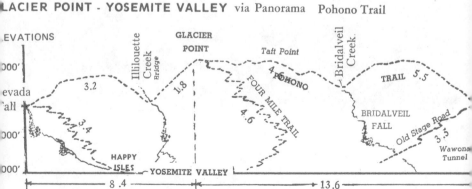

LACIER POINT - YOSEMITE VALLEY via Panorama   Pohono Trail

Upper and lower Yosemite Falls late in the season. Yosemite Creek Trail follows up the ancient stream bed west of the falls to the North Rim trail and Ten Lakes Basin.

NORTH VALLEY RIM TRAILS

YOSEMITE FALLS CREST (6,525′): Total miles—3.3, Time—all day, and **YOSEMITE POINT (6,935′):** Total miles—4.2, Time—all day.

Trail affords a real close-up of the foot of Upper Yosemite Fall. It then ascends many switchbacks up the ancient stream bed before Yosemite Creek was blocked by a great landslide to change its course to plunge over the granite wall. Approach the crest of the upper fall with care. Keep out of the stream above the fall. Yosemite Point is reached by continuing on across the creek and around the canyon rim about 1.0 mi. (It is about 14.0 mi. to Mirror Lake from the crest of Yosemite Falls via the north rim route.)

EAGLE PEAK (7,773′): Total miles—6.1, Time—all day.

From the junction near the crest of Yosemite Falls the route follows up the west side of Yosemite Creek .5 mi. to the Eagle Peak-El Capitan Trail junction. From there it is 2.8 mi. to the summit of Eagle Peak.

SNOW CREEK FALL: Total miles—1.6, Time—½ day.

After leaving the Tenaya Lake Trail the route follows along level Valley floor near Tenaya Creek about 1.0 mi. Falls are at their best early in season. Note: there is no sign to mark the trail.

NORTH DOME (7,531′): Total miles—9.0, Time—all day.

This trip offers excellent views of all the high country that slopes into the main canyon at Yosemite Valley.

To visit the area along the north rim of the canyon some go by car or bus around the Tioga Pass Road to such points as Yosemite Creek or Porcupine Flat and then hike down through this area to the Valley floor.

Other easy one-to-three day trips can be worked out along the many trails leading to special points of interest along the north rim of the Valley, such as the crest of El Capitan, Eagle Peak, crest of upper Yosemite Falls, North Dome, and Indian Rock. By starting at the lower end of the Valley and following the Old Gentry Stage Road up to the west end of El Capitan Trail, one can then travel east to include all these points of interest and return to the Valley via the Tenaya Zig-Zags and Mirror Lake.

Rockslides on the Old Gentry Road cover the trail at one point and make for difficult going. The old road is not maintained or marked as a trail, but can be used as one.

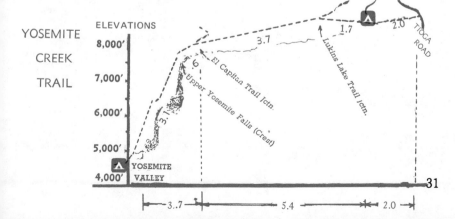

Half Dome & Clouds Rest

South-to-North View
(No Scale)

VIEW OF HALF DOME
FROM CLOUDS REST

HALF DOME
8,852

TUOLUMNE MEADOWS

TENAYA LAKE

SUNRISE MOUNTAIN
9,000

CLOUDS REST
9,924

CLOUDS REST TRAIL
8,250

2.4
8,000
1.8

1.8

MUIR TRAIL

3.3

3.2

CLOUDS REST
7,200

JOHN MUIR TRAIL

7,100

SPRING

HALF DOME TRAIL
2.0

SUNRISE CR.

LITTLE YOSEMITE

1.5

MERCED LAKE

MERCED RIVER

6,000

.5

LOST LAKE

LIBERTY CAP
7,072

6,250

5,900

NEVADA FALL 594'

ANCIENT STREAM COURSES

MT. BRODERICK
6,705

BRIDGE T

EMERALD T

HAPPY ISLES

MIRROR LAKE
4,082

Merced River Canyon Trails

NPS PHOTO

    Both hikers and saddle parties find these trips to be very exciting and well worth the time and effort it takes to get there. Good overnight camping is available in Lower Little Yosemite. Be sure to check with the Park Headquarters for your Wilderness Permit. Tennis shoes or composition soles are best to wear as some parts of the trail are slippery over slick rocks.

    The chain of cables helping the hiker up Half Dome is made up of a series of pipe uprights set in the rock to support the cables hung waist-high on each side of the trail. The top of the dome is a very large, flat area. There are some very slick places that drop off abruptly, so use care when exploring around.

    The face of Clouds Rest, extending into the bottom of Tenaya Canyon, 4500 feet below, is one of the largest continuous rock slopes in the world. It is truly an impressive view of the great solid granite base that lies just below the wooded slopes and flower-checkered meadows.

Note: NEVER attempt to descend to the Valley floor down from the face of Tenaya Canyon.

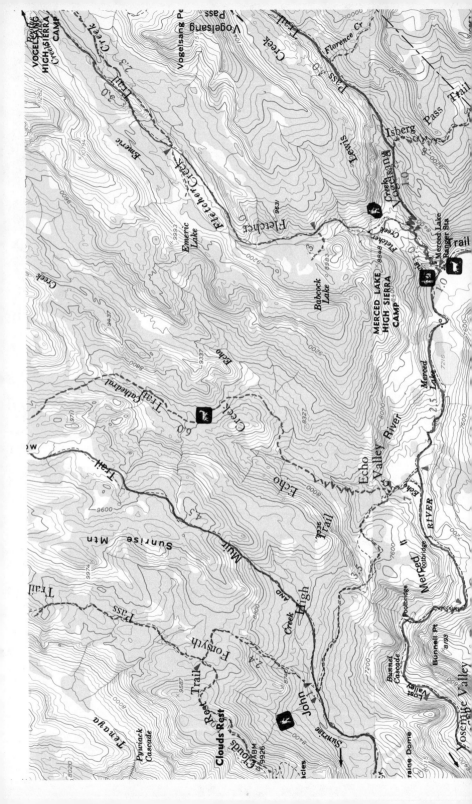

WASHBURN LAKE

NPS PHOTO

Merced River Trails

A trip into this broad river basin becomes an exploration of an ever-changing environment with waterfalls, huge domes, lakes, wooded canyon floors, and glacial-worn walls. Constant companion to the traveler is the River. Everywhere one is exposed to the sounds of cascades, falls, and swift running water. Only in the quiet, shaded depths of Lost Valley do we escape from it for a time.

In this sheltered, deep turn in the canyon, the rich soils have supported an unusual forest of cedar and fir. Above there the trail crosses the river via two bridges. Between the bridges and Echo Flat the route crosses a broad, glacier-swept area littered with erratic boulders. The few mossy banks are fed by springs most of the summer, with numerous quaking aspen and a multitude of moisture-loving plants such as ferns, long-stemmed columbine, and leopard lilies.

At Echo Flat trails lead north to the Sunrise-Cathedral Country. A lateral leads along the high shoulder above Lost Valley to a junction with the John Muir Trail near Sunrise Creek. Before the bridges were built across the river, this High Trail was the main route between Happy Isles and Merced Lake. It is still a favorite route down the canyon in late summer.

At Merced Lake there is a campground, Ranger Station, and a High Sierra Camp where supplies in limited quantity can be secured during the summer: Report in at the Ranger Station your route and be advised where to camp. About two miles up the river is beautiful Washburn Lake, a favorite place to fish and camp.

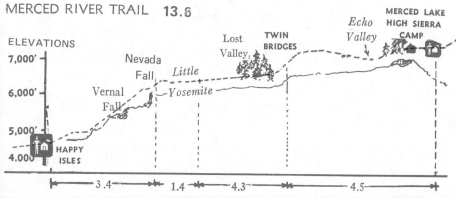

MERCED RIVER TRAIL 13.6

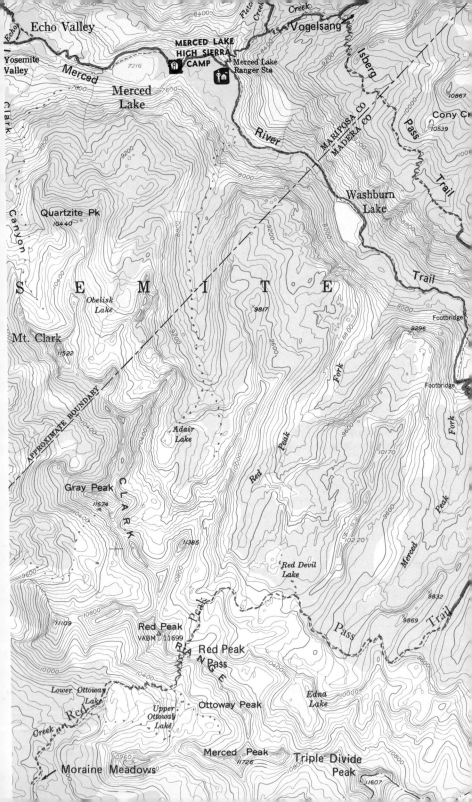

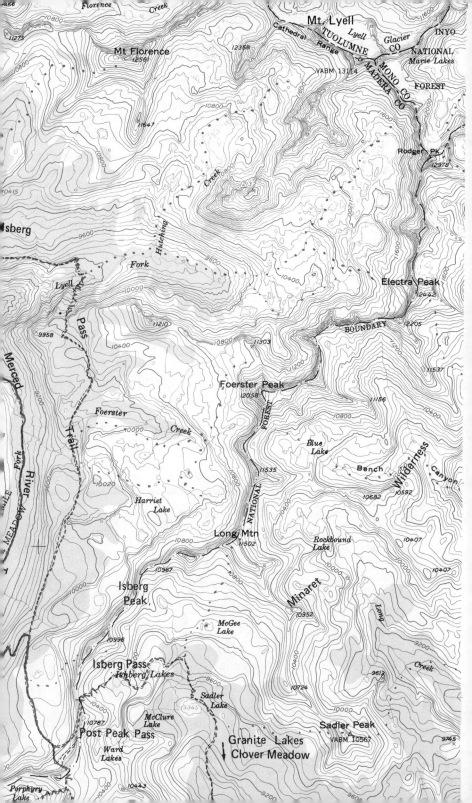

Upper Merced River Basin

Some of the most spectacular scenery in the Park is found in this area. Its highlights include the vast, sweeping panorama to the east that can be seen from Post Peak and Red Peak passes; the canyon of the Lyell Fork of the Merced with its dashing cascades; and the beautiful lakes among the many great granite peaks 10,000 feet to 13,000 feet elevation. A good hike is into the Gray Peak Fork canyon under the east crest of the Clark Range to lovely Adair Lake.

The Red Peak Pass Trail is a magnificent trip. It should not be attempted until the deep snows are cleared from the trail north of the pass. From Red Peak there is a breathtaking view of Mt. Ritter and the Minarets to the east. There are excellent camping sites along the way. Some of the best are at Ottoway Lake, the crossing of the Merced Peak Fork, Ten Mile Meadow, and Triple Peak Fork where the trail junctions with the Merced River Trail. (Be sure to check with the Park Ranger as to what is available when you get your Wilderness Permit.)

MERCED LAKE — POST PEAK PASS—15.0
(via Merced River Trail)

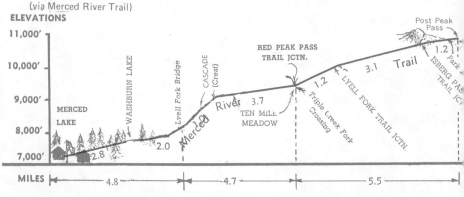

CLARK RANGE FROM ISBERG TRAIL   NPS PHOTO

RED PEAK AND OTTOWAY LAKE   NPS PHOTO

One of the most scenic, remote, high level trips in the Park can be made between Merced Lake Ranger Station and the head of the Merced River Canyon by way of the Vogelsang Pass and Lyell Fork trails. (The Lyell Fork Trail was formerly known as the Isberg Pass Trail.)

RED PEAK PASS TRAIL

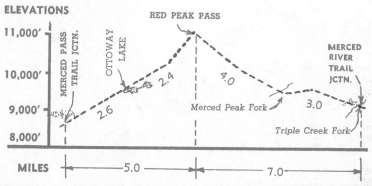

LYELL FORK OF THE MERCED

This trail junctions with the Vogelsang Pass Trail about two miles above the Ranger Station after a climb up switchbacks of some 2000 feet passing steep canyon walls through groves of mountain hemlock to an elevation of about 9500 feet. The trail then levels off along the east rim of the Merced River Canyon. On this ridge there are unusual panoramic views of the whole upper basin of the Merced River framed by the Clark Range to the west, the Triple Divide crest to the south and the Mt. Lyell-Foerster peaks to the east.

In the Lyell Fork canyon the trail is rough and in some places blocked by down trees. Inquiry should be made at the Merced Lake Ranger Station before attempting this route with stock. The upper Lyell Fork canyon lies under the south crest of Mt. Lyell enclosing several small, beautiful lakes near the sheer granite walls. It is a deep glacial trough at about 6000 and 7000 feet elevation surrounded by a great crescent of rocky crags and peaks culminating in Forester Peak (12,062 feet), Electra Peak (12,462 feet), Rodgers Peak (13,036 feet), and at its head Mt. Lyell (13,096 feet).

Cross-country trips can be made and experienced backpacking mountaineers will find much to satisfy them along the Clark Range-Triple Divide crest. There are many high peaks to climb and enough rugged terrain to make these trips a real challenge.

Because of general trail and weather conditions, trips along these high mountain pass routes should be made after the middle of July. Then, most of the snow is gone, meadows are well developed, and the streams are down and clear to provide the best fishing conditions.

The best campsites in the upper valley are about a mile and a half above the trail where Hutchins Creek junctions the Lyell Fork. The real attraction of this area lies in the remote, sublime beauty of these peaks and lakes and views that extend north as far as Mt. Conness, east to the Minarets, south over the broad San Joaquin River Basin, and west to the Clark Range and Fernandez Pass country.

NPS PHOTO

TRIPLE DIVIDE PEAK AND UPPER MERCED RIVER CANYON   NPS PHOTO

MERCED LAKE — ISBERG PASS 10.9
(via Lyell Fork of the Merced Trail)

ELEVATIONS

Foerster Creek

MERCED RIVER TRAIL JCTN.

LYELL FORK CROSSING

VOGELSANG PASS TRAIL JCTN.

FLETCHER CREEK TRAIL JCTN.

MERCED LAKE R.S.

11,000'
10,000'
9,000'
8,000'
7,000'

1.0   1.0   .8   3.0   .5   .6   5.0

2.0   4.3   5.6

South Boundary Country

The South Boundary Country extends from the Wawona-Yosemite highway eastward to the Sierra crest and from the Merced River Canyon south to the headwaters of the San Joaquin River. It includes the watershed basins of Bridalveil Creek, Illilouette Creek, the headwaters of the Merced River, and the South Fork of the Merced River. Its boundary crests and those along the Clark Range enclose a vast landscape that is softened by its covering of miles upon miles of magnificent trees and flowered meadows.

Here is found the unfolding story of the many adaptations of living things to their environment. In the north and central regions of the Park the broad granite basins and glacial torn ridges emphasize the slow, evolutionary changes through eons of time, and the barren landscapes leave one with a feeling of vastness and loneliness. In contrast, the southern part of the Park portrays both an intimacy and warmth as one finds each small cluster of flower with its busy, winged visitor, each meadow and patch of brush with its well-used animal trails, and each tree offering shelter and feed to squirrels and birds.

Not only is this region the home of the giant sequoia, but also here are many other large trees such as the sugar and yellow pines and the red, white and Douglas firs. There are many varieties of broadleaved trees such as oaks, maples, and aspens; also shrubs such as dogwood, manzanita, deer brush, and azalea, all providing interest in form and color with the changing seasons.

Each time of the year has its special attraction for the visitor. In the spring the snowplant and dogwood herald the awakening of the forest from winter's sleep. Summer brings the flower-decked mountain meadows, turbulent open streams lined with fragrant azaleas, and the return of wildlife to the high country. Autumn or Indian Summer splashes the leaves with color and creates feverish activity among the woodfolk in the race to fill their storehouses before winter wraps its mantle over all making it a crystal-white fairyland enjoyed by the lively chickaree and venturesome skier.

This is the only part of the Park open to visitors all year. In winter, Badger Pass is the center of sports activities known for its excellent skiing facilities. In summer, those traveling by car will find easy access to unusual points of interest: the immense panoramic view from either the Glacier Point or Wawona areas, and the gigantic trees in the Mariposa Grove of Sequoias. There are many well marked trails that lead into the backcountry where skyline crests wait to be photographed and lofty peaks challenge the mountain climber.

Hikers into the high country will find best camping conditions between the middle of June and the last of September. The areas around Wawona and the lower Illilouette Basin are the first to open in the early summer, then the region between Glacier Point and Wawona clears, and last, the snow melts on the high mountain passes along the southeast Park boundary and the crest of the Clark Range.

43

Pioneer Yosemite History Center

The old covered bridge invites your entry into the past. For more than 100 years it has marked the comings and goings of miners and settlers, foresters and Presidents, stockmen and tourists. Exhibits include old wagons and about a dozen buildings from Yosemite's pioneer days. Once scattered throughout Yosemite, they were moved here in 1957 to give today's visitors a reconstructed view of what was once a part of that way of life.

Wawona was on the main route of stage coaches and wagons carrying tourists and supplies into Yosemite. They stopped here to rest, repair wagons, and engage in some sight-seeing that usually included a trip up to the "Big Trees", as they were called then.

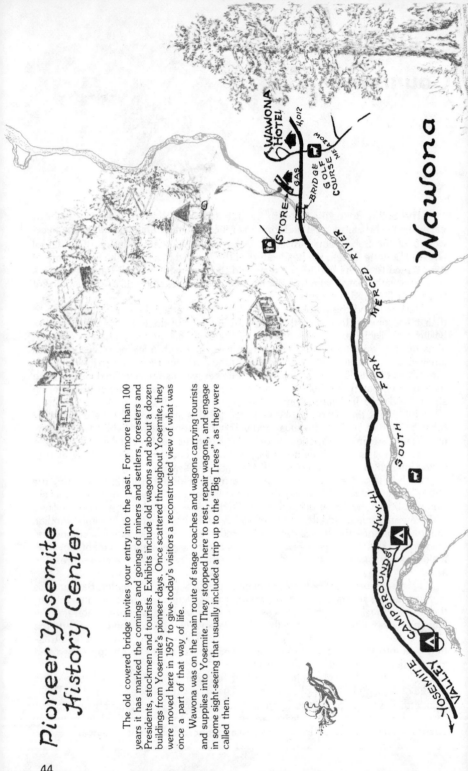

WAWONA-MARIPOSA GROVE AREA

Situated at the edge of an open forest area, Wawona was appropriately named by the Indians—*Wa-wo-nah*—meaning, "Big Tree". Many types of large pines and firs cover the watershed of the South Fork of the Merced River that runs through the valley. Also, in this great forest community are oaks, dogwoods, and alders, complementing their larger, more spectacular neighbors.

Facilities include an all-year campground, Hotel, service station, store, golf course, pack station, post office, and the Pioneer Yosemite History Center.

Wawona is the entrance to some of the most beautiful backcountry of the Sierra extending east to its crest and over to the Devils Postpile. Among the many things to do here, besides fishing along the river, are trips to Chilnualna Falls, a foaming series of cataracts and cascades; Devil's Peak (Signal Peak Lookout); Wawona Point, for a panorama of the entire southern Merced River basin; and a visit to the Mariposa Grove.

The Grove is about three miles east of the south boundary Entrance Station. There is a trail about four miles long between the big trees. Free, open-top shuttle buses take you on a conducted tour through the Grove. If you prefer, you can ride the bus part way and then walk along the trails at your leisure to fully enjoy these magnificent giants.

Wilderness Permits for backcountry trips starting at Wawona may be obtained at the Ranger Station there.

NPS PHOTO

Story of the Sequoias

Neither size nor time can accurately measure the wonder of these woodland giants whose lives extend back into the faint dawn of civilization. Being among the largest and oldest living things they encounter nothing to which they can be compared to except the glacier-quarried mountains that surround their home.

There are three groves of giant sequoias in the Park. THE MARIPOSA GROVE, located near the south entrance of the Park, contains 250 acres that support more than two hundred trees ten feet or more in diameter and a possible 25,000 young trees varying in size from a few inches to 100 feet high. THE TUOLUMNE GROVE, located on the Big Oak Flat Road about one-half mile northwest of Crane Flat and THE MERCED GROVE two miles west of Crane Flat, contain some 25-30 acres each of young and mature trees.

These giant trees are closely related to the "redwoods" along the coast of California and Oregon and the "dawn redwood" of Asia. They grow in sheltered basins at elevations of 5000' to 8500' on the west slopes of the Sierra Nevada and are probably the remains of very extensive forests of such trees that were mostly destroyed during the last Ice Age.

Although few in number, as compared with the oaks, pines, and firs, the sequoias have a remarkable ability to reproduce in warm, sunny areas with rich mineral soil. Each cone contains 150-300 seeds and requires two seasons to mature properly. After opening and releasing their tiny seeds, each weighing less than 1/7000 of an ounce, the empty cone may hang on the tree for many years.

Several methods have been employed to determine the age of trees: cutting across one that has fallen to expose and count its growth rings; boring cores into living trees; and estimating age by comparison. By actual ring count many trees have been found to be more than 3000 to 4000 years old. It is believed that the Grizzly Giant is about 3800 years old. The accompanying diagram presents a graphic story of the possible size in diameter of a giant sequoia in relation to various episodes in human history.

AGE OF THE SEQUOIAS

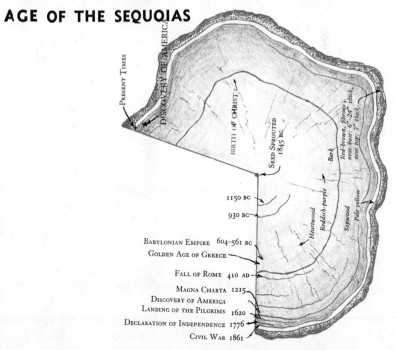

PRESENT TIMES

DISCOVERY OF AMERICA

BIRTH OF CHRIST

SEED SPROUTED 1845 BC

Bark

Red-brown, fibrous; near base; 6"–24" thick; near top; 2" thick

1150 BC

930 BC

Heartwood

Reddish-purple

Sapwood

Pale yellow

BABYLONIAN EMPIRE   604–561 BC
GOLDEN AGE OF GREECE
FALL OF ROME   410 AD
MAGNA CHARTA   1215
DISCOVERY OF AMERICA
LANDING OF THE PILGRIMS   1620
DECLARATION OF INDEPENDENCE   1776
CIVIL WAR   1861

47

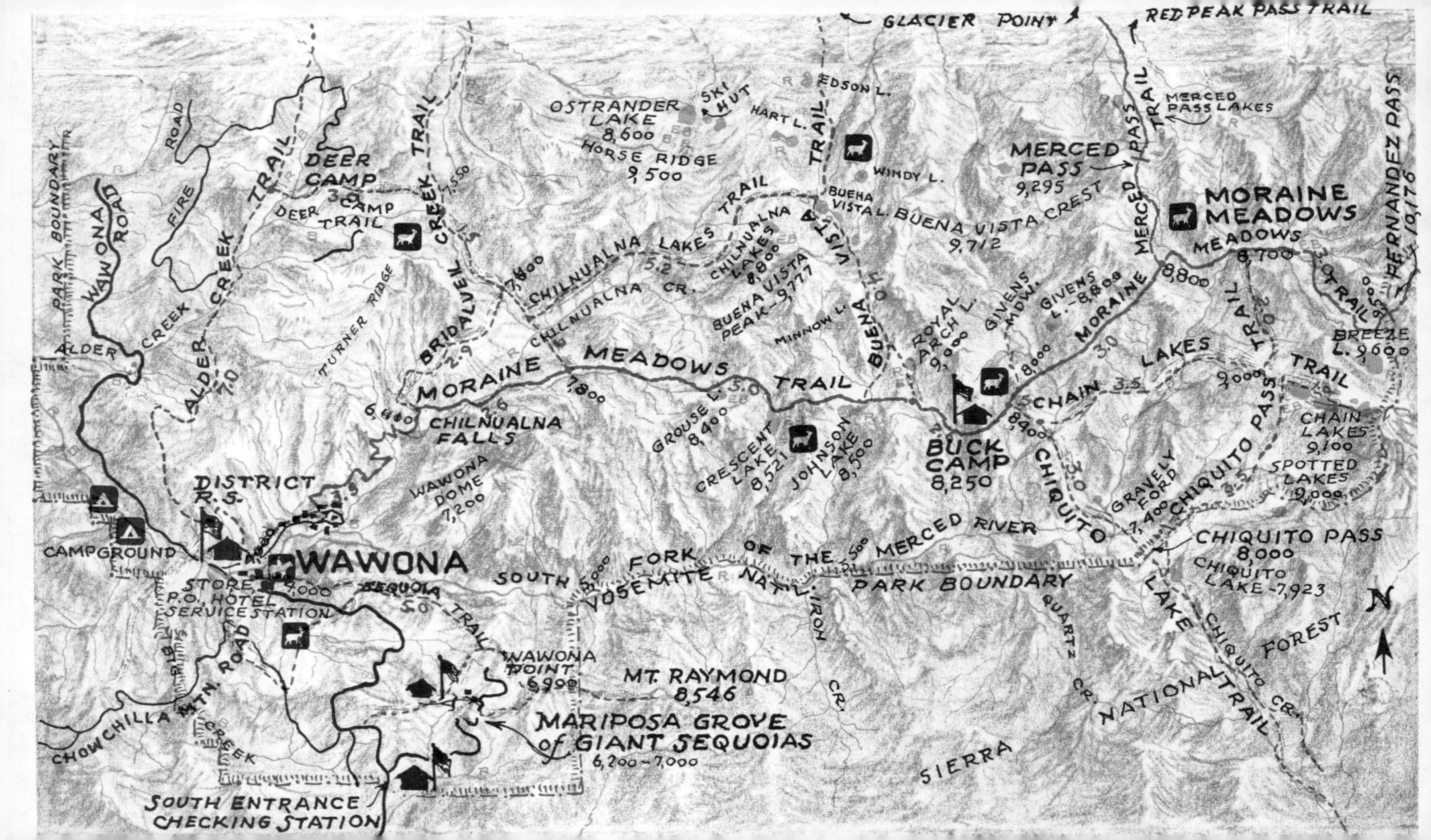
GLACIER POINT
RED PEAK PASS TRAIL
PARK BOUNDARY
WAWONA ROAD
ROAD
FIRE
CREEK
TRAIL
DEER CAMP
3.0
DEER CAMP TRAIL
CREEK
TRAIL
7,550
ALDER CREEK
ALDER
7.0
TURNER RIDGE
BRIDALVEIL
2.9
OSTRANDER LAKE 8,600
SKI HUT
HORSE RIDGE 9,500
HART L.
EDSON L.
TRAIL
WINDY L.
7,800
CHILNUALNA LAKES TRAIL
5.2
CHILNUALNA CR.
CHILNUALNA LAKES 8,800
BUENA VISTA L.
BUENA VISTA PEAK - 9,777
BUENA VISTA CREST 9,712
VISTA
4.0
BUENA
MINNOW L.
MERCED PASS 9,295
MERCED PASS TRAIL
MERCED PASS LAKES
MORAINE MEADOWS
MEADOWS 8,700
FERNANDEZ PASS 10,176
TRAIL
3.0
9,500
8,800
MORAINE
GIVENS MDW.
GIVENS L. - 8,800
ROYAL ARCH L. 9,000
8,000
3.0
BREEZE L. 9,600
LAKES
TRAIL
2.0
TRAIL
MORAINE MEADOWS TRAIL
2.6
5.0
7,800
6,400
CHILNUALNA FALLS
GROUSE L. 8,400
CRESCENT LAKE 8,521
JOHNSON LAKE 8,500
BUCK CAMP 8,250
CHAIN 3.5
8,400
9,000
CHIQUITO PASS
CHAIN LAKES 9,100
SPOTTED LAKES 9,000
3.5
CHIQUITO
3.0
GRAVELY FORD 7,400
CHIQUITO PASS 8,000
CHIQUITO LAKE - 7,923
DISTRICT R.S.
1.5
WAWONA DOME 7,200
CAMPGROUND
WAWONA
4,000
STORE, P.O., HOTEL SERVICE STATION
SEQUOIA
5.0
TRAIL
SOUTH
5,000
FORK
OF THE
5,500
MERCED RIVER
YOSEMITE NAT'L.
PARK BOUNDARY
IRON CR.
QUARTZ CR.
LAKE
TRAIL
CHIQUITO CR.
NATIONAL
FOREST
SIERRA
N
BIG
ROAD
CHOWCHILLA MTN.
CREEK
WAWONA POINT 6,900
MT. RAYMOND 8,546
MARIPOSA GROVE of GIANT SEQUOIAS
6,200 - 7,000
SOUTH ENTRANCE CHECKING STATION

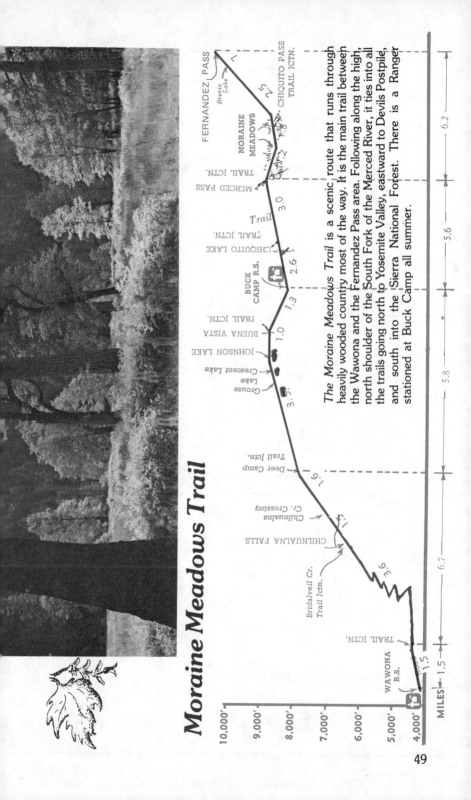

Moraine Meadows Trail

The *Moraine Meadows Trail* is a scenic route that runs through heavily wooded country most of the way. It is the main trail between the Wawona and the Fernandez Pass area. Following along the high, north shoulder of the South Fork of the Merced River, it ties into all the trails going north to Yosemite Valley, eastward to Devils Postpile, and south into the Sierra National Forest. There is a Ranger stationed at Buck Camp all summer.

FERNANDEZ PASS
Breeze Lake
2.5
CHIQUITO PASS TRAIL JCTN.
MORAINE MEADOWS
1.8
1.2
MERCED PASS TRAIL JCTN.
3.0
Trail
CHIQUITO LAKE TRAIL JCTN.
2.6
BUCK CAMP R.S.
1.3
BUENA VISTA TRAIL JCTN.
1.0
JOHNSON LAKE
Crescent Lake
Grouse Lake
.3
Deer Camp Trail Jctn.
1.6
Chilnualna Cr. Crossing
1.1
CHILNUALNA FALLS
3.6
Bridalveil Cr. Trail Jctn.
TRAIL JCTN.
1.5
WAWONA R.S.
.6

10,000'
9,000'
8,000'
7,000'
6,000'
5,000'
4,000'

MILES 1.5 — 6.7 — 5.8 — 5.6 — 6.2

49

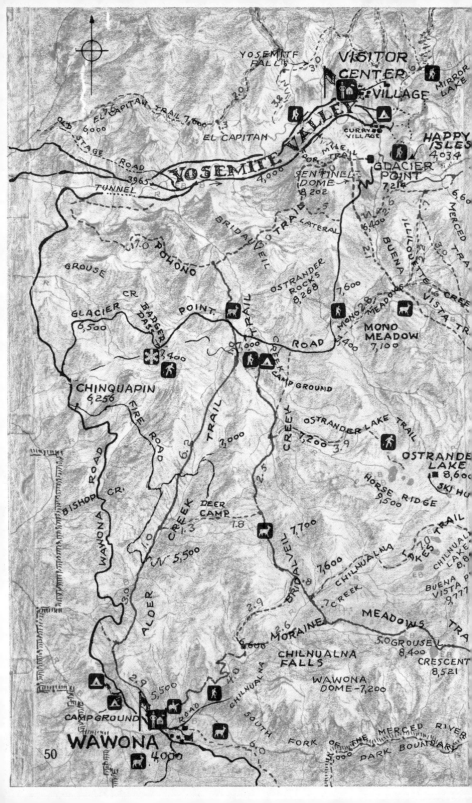

Alder Creek
Bridalveil Creek Basins

Both of these trails are interesting routes between Wawona and Yosemite Valley. Some hikers prefer the Moraine Meadows-Bridalveil Creek route as it gives a general feeling of traveling in a higher, more remote region.

Along the Alder Creek Trail the country is more open and at a lower, drier elevation. In a few places the trail follows along an old abandoned railroad grade used by logging trains in the early days. Campsites will vary somewhat with the season so check with the Ranger Station before starting a trip through here.

Because of its open, southern exposure, this region is noted also as a winter recreational area with cross-country trips to Ostrander Lake from Badger Pass.

WAWONA - POHONO TRAIL JCTN. - 15,1

ALDER CREEK TRAIL

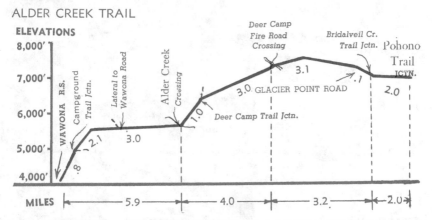

WAWONA - BRIDALVEIL CREEK CAMPGROUND - 14.2

BRIDALVEIL CREEK TRAIL

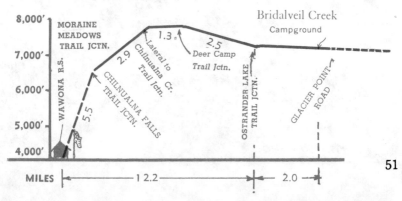

YOSEMITE VALLEY

HALF DOME
8937

JOHN MUIR TRAIL 1.9

LITTLE YOSEMITE

MERCED RIVER

MERCED LAKE
7,250

2.6

GLACIER POINT
7,214

HAPPY ISLES
4034

NEVADA FALL
5,900

MT. CLARK
11,506

3,100

GRAY PK.
11,581

TRAIL

ILLILOUETTE CREEK

GLACIER POINT ROAD

7,600

BUENA VISTA TRAIL

7,000

MERCED PASS TRAIL

GRAYLING L.

ILLILOUETTE

MONO MEADOW
7,100

7,406

2.8

OTTOWAY LAKES
8,886

RED PEAK PASS TRAIL

8.7

OSTRANDER LAKE—8,600

EDSON L.

MERCED PASS LAKES

RED PEAK PASS

3.9

HART LAKE

MERCED PASS—9,295

HORSE RIDGE
9,500

CHILNUALNA LAKES TRAIL

WINDY L.

8,500

BUENA VISTA L.

CREST

MORAINE MEADOW
8,700

3.2

CHILNUALNA LAKES
8,800

BUENA VISTA
9,712

HOOVER L.

BUENA VISTA PASS 9,500

ROYAL ARCH LAKE—9,000

GIVENS MDW.

GIVENS L.—8,000

TRAIL

.7

MINNOW L.

MORAINE

5.0

GROUSE L.

CRESCENT LAKE

JOHNSON LAKE

9,000

BUCK CAMP
8.2
2.6

CHAIN LAKES TRAIL

CHIQUITO PASS TRAIL

3.5

GIVENS CR.

CHIQUITO CR.

CHIQUITO PASS
8,000

CHIQUITO LAKE

SOUTH FORK OF THE MERCED

YOSEMITE PARK BOUNDARY

5,000

IRON CR.

QUARTZ CR.

CHIQUITO CR.

CHIQUITO LAKE TRAIL

52

MT. RAYMOND
8,546

Illilouette Basin

Entry into this broad, wooded basin is best made from Glacier Point or Mono Meadows, thereby avoiding the long, steep climb up out of the Valley. Mono Meadows is located between Glacier Point Road and Illilouette Creek. The Illilouette Basin includes miles upon miles of gentle, wooded slopes abounding in wildlife.

The Buena Vista and Merced Pass trails provide easy access to this beautiful region making a good loop trip for those not hardened to difficult mountain trails. An alternate trip could be made returning by way of Red Peak Pass and the Merced River Canyon Trail.

This seldom visited region with its small streams, broad meadows and lakes famous for fishing is ideal camping country.

JOHNSON LAKE - GLACIER POINT: - 15.5 ——— *Buena Vista Trail*

MORAINE MEADOWS - NEVADA FALL: - 15.0 • • • • *Merced Pass Trail*

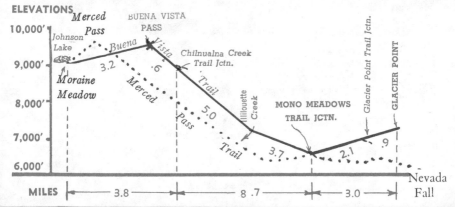

ELEVATIONS

ILLILOUETTE BASIN   NPS PHOTO

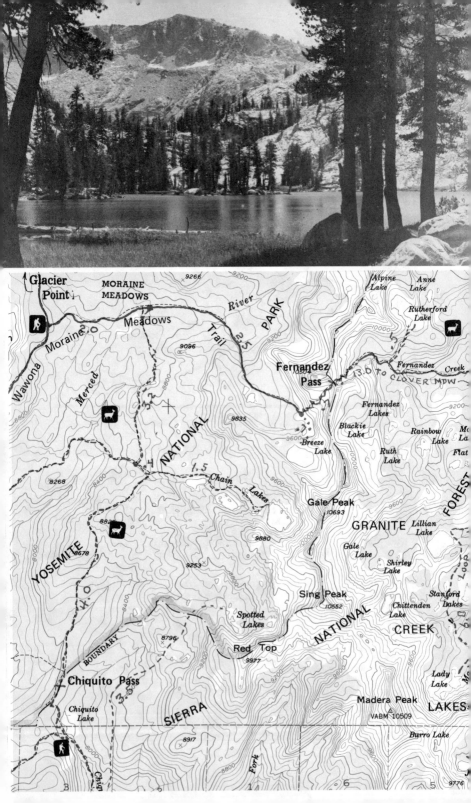

Minarets Wilderness

Immediately adjacent to Yosemite National Park, along its southeast boundary, lies the Minarets Wilderness. South boundary country hikers will find this region unusual in its offering of numerous well-stocked lakes and ideal camping conditions. Extended loop trips out of the Park into the Granite Lakes area (via Fernandez Pass) are most rewarding. Both scenery and lake fishing are good to the south and east of Post Peak Pass or Isberg Pass as is the remote upper basin headwaters of the North Fork of the San Joaquin.

Between Chiquito Pass and Fernandez Pass the high-walled backdrop of the eastern Park boundary provides a magnificent setting for many lakes where fishing and scenic settings are superb. In this remote corner of the Park trail traffic is light and extensive wooded areas invite early season camping. Just beyond the boundary the many lakes of Granite Creek can be reached by excellent trails out from the Beasore Meadow-Clover Meadows road.

HEMLOCK CROSSING   "BUTCH" JONES, USFS, MINARETS

Minarets Road: Extends from North Fork to Clover Meadow. Paved most of the way. Offers spectacular views up the broad San Joaquin River basin to the eastern Sierra crest and the Kaiser Crest to the south.

Between Oakhurst and Fish Camp the Sky Ranch, Sugarpine, and Big Sandy roads lead in to the Nelder Grove of Sequoias and the forest region lying between the Minarets Road and the southern boundary of Yosemite National Park. Most of these are gravel base or dirt roads that have been developed along the old logging train grades of early days when extensive areas of firs, pines, and sequoias were cut. Sugarpine had a large sawmill operation. After the logs were sawed the rough boards were bound and hooked together into "trains". These were dumped into flumes that carried them many miles to another mill near Madera. Interesting reminders of those early days of Sugarpine are found at the Railroad Museum.

Minarets Country

Tuolumne Meadows

Mt. McCLURE

MT. LYELL

DONOHUE PASS
11,050

Rush Creek

Gem Lake

Agnew Lake

Waugh Lake

Island Pass

AGNEW PASS

SAN JOAQUIN MTN

YOSEMITE NATIONAL PARK

Marie Lake

RODGERS PEAK

JOHN

Lyell Fork

Merced River

ELECTRA PEAK

Thousand Island Lake

MT. DAVIS
12,308

MUIR TRAIL

PACIFIC CREST TRAIL

FOERSTER PEAK
12,059

Twin Island Lakes
9600

BANNER PEAK
12,957

Garnet Lake

Yosemite Valley

ISBERG PASS TRAIL

BLUE LAKE BENCH

CANYON 10,00

RITTER PEAK
13,156

Wilderness

Shadow Lake

San Joaquin River

Harriet Lake
10,300

ROCKBOUND LAKE

Stevenson Meadow

RITTER

Agnew Meadow

MERCED RIVER TRAIL

LONG MTN.

Hemlock Crossing

MINARETS RANGE

VOLCANIC RIDGE

San Joaquin Dk

ISBERG PASS
10,500

Minarets

Long Creek

Dike Creek

Minaret Creek

Beck Lakes

POST PEAK PASS
10,600

ISBERG PASS TRAIL 10,10

SADLER PEAK
10,562

STEVENSON TRAIL

NORTH FORK

MINARETS

Iron Creek

DEVILS POSTPILE
7,560

POST PEAK TRAIL

Cora Lakes

East Fork

Lily Lake

WILDERNESS TRAIL

IRON CREEK TRAIL

IRON LAKE

IRON MTN.
11,149

King Creek

Summit Meadow
9,000

MAMMOTH 8.0

TIMBER CREEK TRAIL

TIMBER KNOB
9,963

Post Creek

West Fork

GREEN MTN.
8,600'

Sheep Crossing

SAN JOAQUIN FORK

Granite Stairway
9,200

GRANITE

POSTPILE 8.0

Cargyle Creek

Shake Mdw.

CORRAL

CARGYL MD
8,000

Stairway

RIVER

RAINBOW TRAIL

Granite Creek
Campground
7,000

SOLDIER MEADOW
7,000

SAN JOAQUIN

MIDDLE FORK

SAN JOAQUIN

Fish Creek

CLOVER MEADOW
7,000

CATTLE MTN.
7,915

JUNCTION BUTTE 6,570

JUNCTION BLUFFS

MILLER CROSSING

Caution: Climbing in the Minarets should be done only by well equipped and experienced climbers, and never alone.

MINARETS WILDERNESS

The tremendous encircling horseshoe arms of the Post Peak to Rodgers Peak range to the west and the Ritter Range with its Minarets to the east enclose dozens of high lakes. Most elevations range from 7500' to 9000'. The western crest peaks stand well above 12,000' and the eastern Ritter Range exceeds 13,000'.

Streams and lakes are stocked with rainbow, eastern brook and golden. The best fishing is usually found at Twin Island, Blue or Rockbound lakes. Principal streams in the Wilderness which afford excellent catches are the West and East Forks of Granite Creek and the North Fork of the San Joaquin.

Most of the region is above timberline. In lower elevations are the dense stands of red fir, Jeffrey pine, lodgepole pine, mountain hemlock, and quaking aspen, as well as a wide variety of shrubs and flowers. It is well populated with deer, bear, the whole range of squirrels and chipmunks and many types of birds.

Clover Meadow provides the most central location for backcountry trips into this region. Trailheads along the Beasore Road lead north to the Park boundary from Fresno Dome Camp, Grizzley Creek, Chiquito Pass, Fernandez Pass, Post Peak/Isberg passes, and the Hemlock Crossing on upper North Fork of the San Joaquin. For full information on current roads, trails, and campgrounds check with the Minarets Ranger District at North Fork, CA 93643 (209) 877-2218. Most of the roads are closed between November and late May due to heavy snow, with the exception of snowshoes and extended Nordic skiing ventures.

Mammoth and Devils Postpile provides access to the North Fork Basin lying west of the Ritter Range and the Yosemite south and east boundary country. The route follows the old pioneer Mammoth-Postpile Trail. The ancient native Indians used this trail to trade with the Monos of the Owens Valley country. When gold was discovered at Mammoth this became the route for pack trains carrying supplies from the San Joaquin Valley towns to the "diggings". In later years cattle and sheep men moved their stock in summer to the mountain meadows of the Sierra via Sheep Crossing and 77 Corral.

MT. DAVIS   IRON LAKE   "BUTCH" JONES, USFS, MINARETS

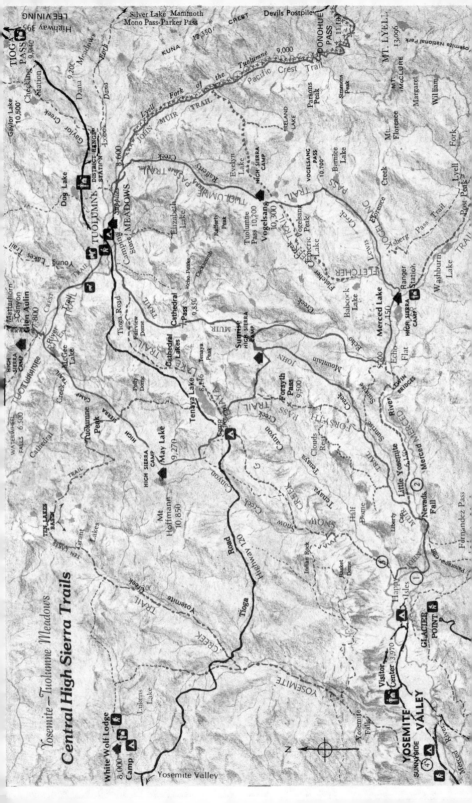

Yosemite–Tuolumne Meadows
Central High Sierra Trails

Central
Sierra Trails

Yosemite Valley and Tuolumne Meadows are the principal trailheads of five major routes across the glorious high country lying between them. Some half dozen lateral trails permit exploration of the area or by shorter loop trips. The varied offerings of the region include a complete spectrum of landforms, forest cover, and wildlife. Principal routes are: (1) JOHN MUIR TRAIL, (2) MERCED RIVER TRAIL, (3) SNOW CREEK-TENAYA LAKE TRAIL, (4) YOSEMITE CREEK-TEN LAKES TRAIL, and (5) HIGH SIERRA CAMP LOOP TRIP.

① JOHN MUIR TRAIL

No more appropriate place than Happy Isles could be found for the northern entry to the wilderness country between Yosemite and Mt. Whitney, 212 miles south. It was in this Valley's meadows and near its streams and falls that John Muir dwelt upon the mysteries of the great forces of nature that built these mountains.

He was a self-taught naturalist who was the first to recognize and report the glacial action responsible for the "Range of Light"—his name for the great Sierra which he called the most hospitable and finest mountain range in all the world.

Because of his unbounded love of nature, he devoted most of his life to the preservation of our wilderness areas and was a prime instigator in securing the creation of the Yosemite National Park by Congress in 1890.

A trip along Yosemite's portion of the John Muir Trail will reward the traveler with far reaching vistas, the association with tumultuous streams, the quiet of wooded basins, and the chance encounter with many kinds of wildlife that make this area their home.

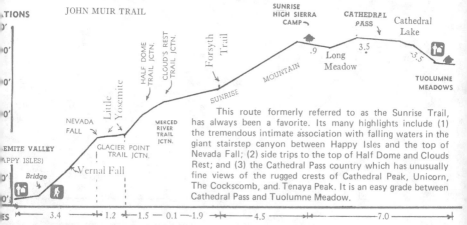

This route formerly referred to as the Sunrise Trail, has always been a favorite. Its many highlights include (1) the tremendous intimate association with falling waters in the giant stairstep canyon between Happy Isles and the top of Nevada Fall; (2) side trips to the top of Half Dome and Clouds Rest; and (3) the Cathedral Pass country which has unusually fine views of the rugged crests of Cathedral Peak, Unicorn, The Cockscomb, and Tenaya Peak. It is an easy grade between Cathedral Pass and Tuolumne Meadow.

② MERCED RIVER TRAIL

This route is somewhat longer than the Muir Trail between Tuolumne Meadows and Happy Isles. It does, however, make a most satisfactory change of mountain trail as it follows close to the Merced River from Happy Isles to Merced Lake. The forested upper Little Yosemite Valley and deep woodsy feeling at Lost Valley are great contrasts to the cascades above the Twin Bridges crossing.

Between Merced Lake to Vogelsang two routes present different environments. The Lewis Creek route passes trails to some half dozen lakes including Florence and Bernice, then makes an easy ascent to Vogelsang Pass, drops down to follow close to Vogelsang Lake and the High Sierra Camp. The Fletcher Creek trail provides fine lake fishing and camping. Passing to the west of towering Vogelsang Peak (11,511') you may be fortunate enough to see an eagle soaring in the updraft along the cliffs.

Time taken to make the ascent to Vogelsang Peak will be most rewarding, in the far reaching panorama of the many eastern basins of the Merced River and north across the vast watershed of the Tuolumne.

From Vogelsang it is an easy down grade trip across open tundra country via Rafferty Creek to Tuolumne.

A more varied offering is found on the Evelyn Lake alternate where trails lead up to Ireland Lake. You can cross country along the east slope of Parsons and Simmons peak where fine views down the Lyell Fork and into the deep glacier filled cirques of McClure and Lyell.

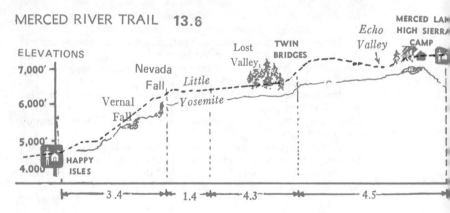

MERCED RIVER TRAIL 13.6

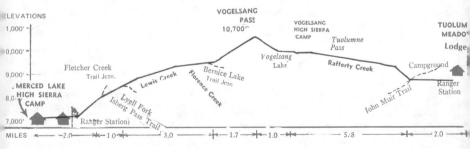

VOGELSANG PASS TRAIL

60

③ TENAYA CANYON

NPS PHOTO

This is the shortest route between Yosemite Valley and Tuolumne Meadows. It leaves the Valley floor above Mirror Lake, ascends the steep Tenaya Zig-Zags and junctions with trails along the North Valley Rim; follows the high north shoulder of Tenaya Canyon across from Half Dome and Clouds Rest to Tenaya Lake, and the dome country between there and Tuolumne Meadows.

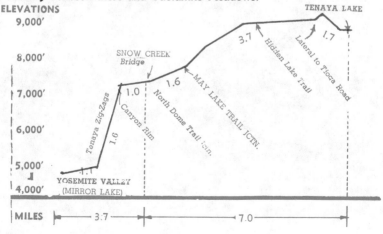

④ YOSEMITE CREEK-TEN LAKES BASIN

Trailhead is at Sunnyside (Walk-In) Campground west of Yosemite Lodge. Ascending the steep canyon wall, it presents a most unusual view of the Valley, the South Valley Rim, and the immensity of Yosemite Falls. Lateral trails lead east and west along the North Valley Rim. The trail follows up the broad basin of upper Yosemite Creek Country culminating in the Ten Lakes Basin.

The Ten Lakes country is rich in scenery, fishing and all around good camping, which is why it is so popular. The region has a special interest to naturalists as it contains evidences of basic plant adaptations at various levels. Aside from the obvious effects of elevation changes, there are many examples of the results of climatic, exposure, and soil conditions. The trail progresses from one typical environment to another and includes stands of lodgepole pine, fir, Jeffrey Pine, and juniper. Trailheads into this area are also along the Tioga Road near the Yosemite Creek crossing and in the Tenaya-May Lake area, or from White Wolf. (Note: there is no camping permitted at Lukens Lake-One Mile Rule)

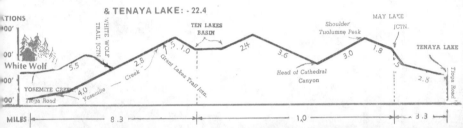

ITE WOLF or YOSEMITE CREEK to TEN LAKES
& TENAYA LAKE: - 22.4

TEN LAKES BASIN

Tuolumne Meadows

TRAILHEAD TO THE YOSEMITE HIGH SIERRA

Of the several trailhead centers in Yosemite National Park, Tuolumne Meadows has always been the favorite of back country bound hikers. The Tioga Road provides access at a high elevation, saving a lot of uphill drag needed to get into the high country from trailheads in the western part of the Park. It makes an ideal departure point with main routes leading to the High Sierra Camps, south to the Postpile or Merced River Canyon, and to Yosemite's North Country.

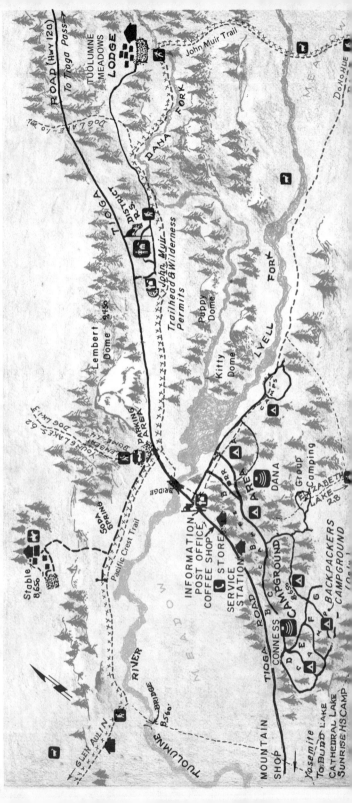

Tuolumne Meadows

Tuolumne Meadows is ideally situated for family groups seeking a High Sierra camping experience. Lying in the heart of the backcountry, it serves as a base camp for hikers making short, one-to-three day trips to the numerous mountain peaks, streams, and lakes nearby, as well as for backpackers making extended journeys into wilderness areas. From here trails branch out to all parts of the eastern and northern areas of the Park.

To appreciate Tuolumne, get away from the road or the campground and walk to a lake, meander through a meadow, climb a peak, or just sit on a rock beside the river and become a part of this great "natural" environment. Enrich your spirits by hearing the birds or the wind whispering through the lodgepoles, by smelling the richness of the earth or by looking at the forces of nature that shaped the landscape around you.

The Park Service operates a large campground for all types of camping. Their full-scale Naturalist program includes conducted walks and hikes, campfire talks, and trip planning services. You can obtain information for your Wilderness Permit, latest trail conditions, a detailed account of what to see and do, and maps from the Backcountry Information Kiosk, located in the large parking area just west of the District Ranger Station. No permits are available at the Visitor Center. Mountaineering parties should check with the Kiosk, not with the District Ranger Headquarters.

The facilities include a Lodge, store (with a good supply of staples), service station, saddle horses, pack station, telephone, post office, and daily bus service during the summer.

Remember, you are above 8000 feet elevation so you may puff a little. Anyone in normal, good health should have no concern about hiking after a day or two of acclimating.

NPS PHOTO

NPS PHOTO

A FEW

RECOMMENDED

TRIPS

With so many lakes and interesting peaks in the Tuolumne area, it is difficult to include them all. As a starter, a few are given here. The first group requires only moderate effort that might well include younger members of the family. Group two is a list of backcountry treks high in quality, moderate in difficulty, that includes some cross-country work and needs two to four days to really get the most out of the area visited.

GROUP ONE (Distances are from Tioga Road. Trailheads: TH:)

1. **Lembert Dome:** 2.0 miles. Moderate climb. Unusual views of Tuolumne Meadows and surrounding peaks. Never attempt a shortcut down the west slope of dome, it is very dangerous. (TH: parking area north of bridge)
2. **Dog Lake:** 1.5 miles. Very easy trip through lodgepole forest and small flowered meadows. Excellent choice to take family for picnic. (TH: parking available at Muir Trail Parking Area on Lodge Road)
3. **Elizabeth Lake:** 2.5-3 miles. (Close to impressive ragged peaks. Charming meadow and forested route. (TH: back of campground)
4. **Cathedral Lakes:** 2.5-3 miles. Tops in High Sierra beauty amid Cathedral peaks and crests. Extensive views. Good fishing. (TH: Western end of meadow-John Muir Trail route)
5. **May Lake:** 1.0-2.0 miles. Easy scenic trail. Lake lies at base of Mt. Hoffman. High Sierra Camp here. (TH: three miles west of Tenaya Lake)
6. **Mt. Dana:** A moderate "walk-up" trek with extensive panorama views. (TH: Tioga Road above Dana Meadows)
7. **Waterwheel Falls:** 16.4 miles round trip from Soda Springs. To be seen at its best go early in the season. The numerous cascades and waterwheel falls make it a very spectacular trip. It is a long, strenuous one-day round trip. To be fully enjoyed, take at least two days.

BACKPACKERS IN CATHEDRAL COUNTRY   EUGENE ROSE

GROUP TWO (Check your route with the Ranger when you get your Permit at the Wilderness Kiosk)

1. **Upper Echo Creek Basin:** Good loop trip to include Cathedral Lakes, cross-country to Echo, Matthes, Nelson, and Raymond lakes. Return via Rafferty Creek or Vogelsang, Ireland lakes and Muir Trail to Tuolumne.

2. **Ireland Lake-Lyell Fork area:** A good beginners trek with some easy cross-country travel to explore upper end of Lyell Fork Canyon near McClure and Lyell Glaciers.

3. **Vogelsang-Gallison Lakes:** Some 15 lakes within a five mile radius in above timberline setting. Easy trails and gradual climbs most cross-country routes.

FOR MOUNTAINEERING ENTHUSIASTS: Distances and time to climb Mt. Lyell, Mt. Dana and Mt. Conness vary with the time of year, routes selected, and the ability of each individual. Each summer Ranger Naturalists conduct regular trips to these peaks. Parties planning to go on their own must check at the Wilderness Kiosk regarding the best routes, weather predictions, and the length of time they expect to be gone.

MT. DANA   ROCKY ROCKWELL

MAY LAKE

ECHO PEAK

CATHEDRAL PEAKS

NPS PHOTOS

THE MT. LYELL EXPERIENCE

The Lyell-Rodgers crest stands at the apex and crossing of a great X of the Cathedral-Ritter Range and the towering peaks forming the eastern boundary of Yosemite National Park between Mt. Dana and Sing Peak. From its summit is gained a full 360° panorama view unequalled anywhere in the northern Sierra.

To the east lies the broad scarred canyons of the ancient Rush Creek glacier that carved out the upper basins now holding the lovely Marie and Gem lakes. The lower, deeper canyons lead northeast carrying the waters of Silver and Grant lakes and Rush Creek to their final rest in Mono Lake.

To the southeast are gathered the waters from the snow and ice fields of the Minaret Crest. The John Muir-Pacific Crest Trail follows along the high shoulder west of the Middle Fork of the San Joaquin. Traversing the shores of Thousand Island, Garnet, and Shadow lakes, it provides easy access to scores of small rockbound lakes that reflect the nearby majesty of Banner, Ritter and the Minarets.

Southward the view covers the whole sweep of the Minarets Wilderness and the entire upper basin of the North and South Forks of the far-reaching San Joaquin. Westward, between the rugged arms of Cathedral Range and Clark Range, lies the headwaters of the mighty Merced. Each of its high granite basins has its own special charm. All combine to tell the story where ancient glaciers formed and began their journey westward to hew out the Little Yosemite, the great waterfall-filled stairstep canyon below Nevada Fall, and Happy Isles. Then, joining forces with the Tenaya Canyon glacier below Half Dome, they carved out the majesty of the "Incomparable Valley".

Along the shaded north walls of Lyell and McClure spreads the Lyell-McClure Glaciers, reminders of the time when these upper basins overflowed with moving fields of glittering ice. So great was its depth, huge arms flowed eastward to form the canyons now known as Parker Creek, Walker Creek, Gibbs Creek, and the LeeVining gorges. The view northwest down the Grand Canyon of the Tuolumne extends across the headwaters of the Tuolumne and eastward to Mt. Conness, the Matterhorn Crest, Sawtooth Ridge and Tower Peak. Truly it is an unusual climax of the northern Sierra where the work of the ages is unfolded in sweeping array.

Most ascents of the mountain have been made from Tuolumne Meadows. Climbers guides list it as Class 2-3 in difficulty. Other routes are from upper Marie Lake (class 3) and the head of Hutchins Creek (class 3-4). From Tuolumne Meadows the north and east approach is best made via the John Muir Trail. Follow up the Lyell Fork Canyon to Middle or Upper Base Camp (9.5 miles) the first day. This allows ample time the second day to climb the peak and return to your base camp. The third day is a leisurely return to Tuolumne Meadows.

Complete information about conducted trips and planning individual group ascents (NEVER ALONE) can be secured at Yosemite Valley or Tuolumne Wilderness Kiosk. Some routes require crampons and an ice axe. From Lyell Base Camp, trips can be extended to include McClure Glacier and several other nearby peaks.

A pleasant trip for the less competent in mountaineering is up the Lyell Fork of the Tuolumne going south on the John Muir Trail. Side trips can be made to Ireland Lake or the northwest rim of the Lyell Glacier, which is not too difficult and provides a truly arctic-alpine experience.

For a longer trip, instead of returning to Tuolumne Meadows, a most exciting, scenic route is to continue over the Donohue Pass on the John Muir Trail going south along the shores of many beautiful lakes that lie beneath the eastern slopes of Banner Peak, Mt. Ritter and the Minarets. The exit from this region can be made at the Agnew Meadows Devils Postpile trailheads.

Upper McCabe Lake

Hess Mine

Steelhead Lake

Twin Lake

Odell Lake

Lundy Pass

"Z" Lake

Hummingbird Lake

Oneida Lake 9656

Hoover

Tioga

Wilderness

Crest

Cliff Cr

Dore Pass

Cascade Lake

Mill

Wasco Lake

INYO

North Peak

12242

Sheep Peak

Greenstone Lake

Conness Lakes

(Natural)

Saddlebag Lake

Roosevelt Lake

Conness Glacier

HALL

Area

NATIONAL

MT. CONNESS

VABM 12590

MONO CO

TUOLUMNE CO

Saddlebag Lake Resort

Gardisky Lake 9777

Alpine Lake

Carnegie Institute Experimental Sta.

NATURAL

Sawmill Campground

Yosemite

Green Treble Lake

Maul Lake

FOREST

Tioga P

Big Horn Lake

Finger Lake

Spuller Lake

Lee Vining Creek

White Mtn

Fantail Lake

Mine

Shell Lake

National

AREA

11200

12002

Skelton Lakes

Bennettville (Site) Tunnel

Creek

Tioga Resort

11255

Great Sierra Mine

10932

BM 9734

Park

Granite Lakes

Gaylor Pk

Creek

Gaylor Lakes

Tioga Pass

10400

10046

Ranger Sta.

9945

Delaney

Moraine Flat

BASE

LINE

Gaylor Lakes Trail

10000

Road

BM 9860

Mt. Dana

Dana Meadows

9600

9697

9200

TIOGA

BM 9038

BM 9151

Tioga

BM 9521

Mono Pass

The upper LeeVining Creek basin lying west of the Saddlebag Lake road has long been by-passed for more advertised areas. Actually, its waters provide some of the finest fishing in this part of the Sierra. Its quiet seclusion from the busy Tioga Road is a welcome surprise. The scenic crest along the White Mountain-Conness Divide includes many small ice-field-fed streams and lakes.

Several campgrounds are on the lower LeeVining Creek and valley road up to the powerhouse, or at Ellery Lake, Tioga Lake, and near Tioga Resort at the junction to the road to Saddlebag. There is a walk-in campground at Sawmill and a real "high" country campground at Saddlebag Lake.

Tioga Resort services include supplies, meals, accommodations, gas station, and fishing information and equipment. The Saddlebag Lake Resort store has groceries and fishing supplies, a boat dock and boat rentals, some meals and information about the area. A boat taxi is available to the upper end of the lake.

Northeast of Tioga Pass and Saddlebag Lake is the Hoover Wilderness. This area includes the headwater basins of LeeVining Creek and Mill Creek. Warren Canyon, outstanding in scenic beauty, has very little traffic.

Another recommended trip is to the Gaylor/Granite Lakes area. Trailhead for the short route to Gaylor is located at Tioga Pass Entrance Station. It is a very steep trail with splendid views south and east. There is a longer route using the Gaylor Lakes Trail about two miles east of Tuolumne on the Tioga Road. It is an easy grade that follows Gaylor Creek up to the lakes. Along the way the small groves of lodgepoles are separated by several small, flower-decked meadows.

NORTH PEAK   ROCKY ROCKWELL PHOTOS

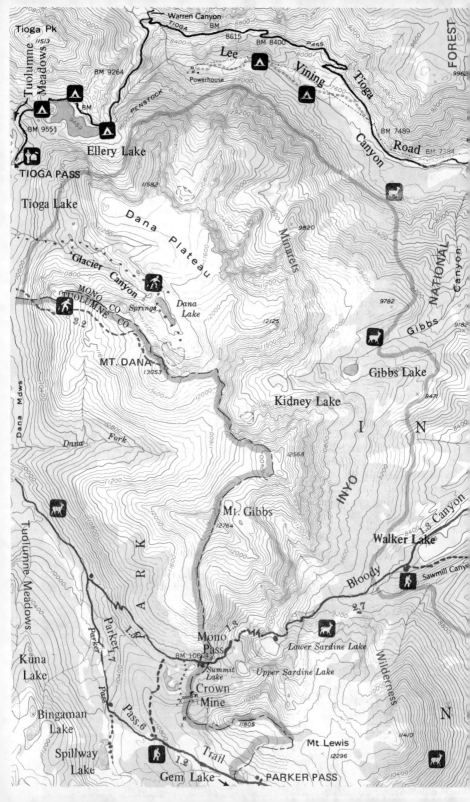

A trip into the region between the east slopes of Kuna Crest and the Park Boundary include several lakes most prominent being Helen and Bingaman. Exit from the Park leading to the June Lake-Silver Lake basin can be made at Parker Pass.

The Parker Pass Trail follows close under the Kuna Peak, Koip Peak, and their glacial fields. The route continues over Koip Pass above the glacier and on down past Alger and Gem Lakes. From here you can go east to the Silver Lake-June Lake trailheads; south to Agnew Meadows and Devils Postpile; west past Waugh Lake to join the John Muir Trail and Pacific Crest Trail to Donohue Pass back into the Park.

Because this is such beautiful country and so accessible, it is extremely popular. Your assistance in caring for this fragile wilderness is vital.

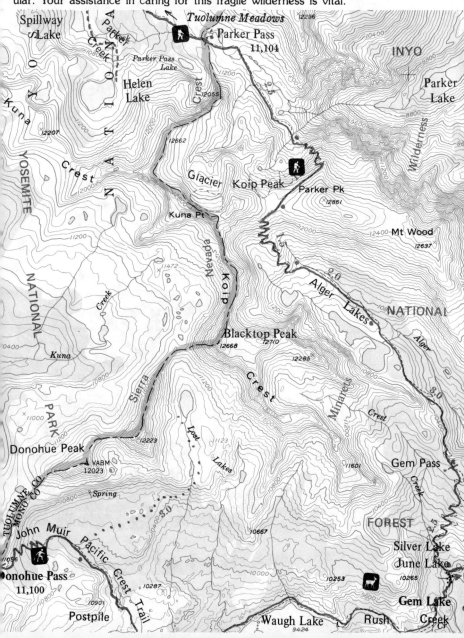

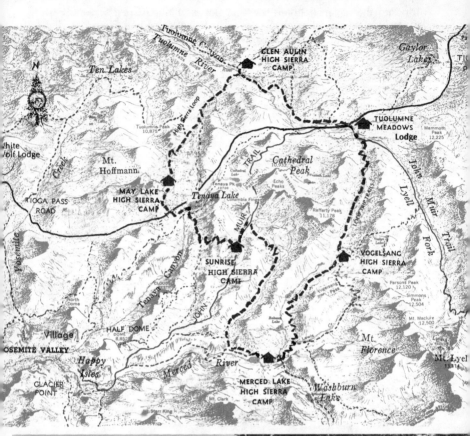

MERCED LAKE CAMP

High Sierra Camps

Long ago the Yosemite's central High Sierra was sought out for its beauty and unusual geological features. First among them was John Muir as he searched for answers about Yosemite's creation, and by scientists and mountaineers trying to unlock the secrets held in the deep canyons and unexplored crests of the central Sierra. The region lay between 8000 and 13,000 feet in elevation and was extremely difficult to penetrate. It contained some of the deepest canyons and highest peaks of the northern Sierra with a climate, vegetation and wildlife typical of the Hudsonian and Alpine environments.

Today's High Sierra camps have been established in areas with concern for the best that the region offers and are all easy, one-day trips. You can go to one or more of them on an individual basis for an overnight stay, or take one of their scheduled trips.

Services at each camp are not limited to those taking these scheduled trips. They include family style meals; hot showers (for a nominal fee); a telephone for emergencies; supplies limited to staple items such as film, tobacco, first aid and some backpackers foods; and managers familiar with the area who are anxious to assist you. For all meals and overnight accommodations and established trips, advance reservations are required.

Each Monday morning a 7-day walking loop trip led by a Park Ranger Naturalist leaves Tuolumne Meadows for Glen Aulin. The Naturalist discusses the environment along the trail and gives campfire programs each night. On this tour there is a two-day lay over at Merced Lake.

There are also two 6-day and two 4-day saddle trips accompanied by an experienced guide. For more information and reservations contact the Yosemite Park & Curry Company at Yosemite Village.

Usually the trips start from Tuolumne Meadows going down to Glen Aulin. However, you can reach May Lake by leaving your car at Snow Flat, off the Tioga Road and walk up to the lake. The Sunrise High Sierra Camp can be reached directly from Tuolumne Meadows via the John Muir Trail; from Tenaya Lake via the Forsyth Pass and Sunrise Lakes Trails; and from Yosemite Valley (Happy Isles) via the John Muir Trail. The Merced Lake and Vogelsang High Sierra camps are available via the John Muir, Merced River, or the Vogelsang Pass trails.

The Tuolumne River Trail to Glen Aulin and on down into the Grand Canyon of the Tuolumne is ideal for those just arriving in the mountains and in need of an easy beginning for a backcountry trip. It follows along open meadows and sparsely wooded sections before dropping down closer to the river canyon walls.

Glen Aulin High Sierra Camp is right below the roaring White Cascades, nestled at the edge of mountain hemlocks.

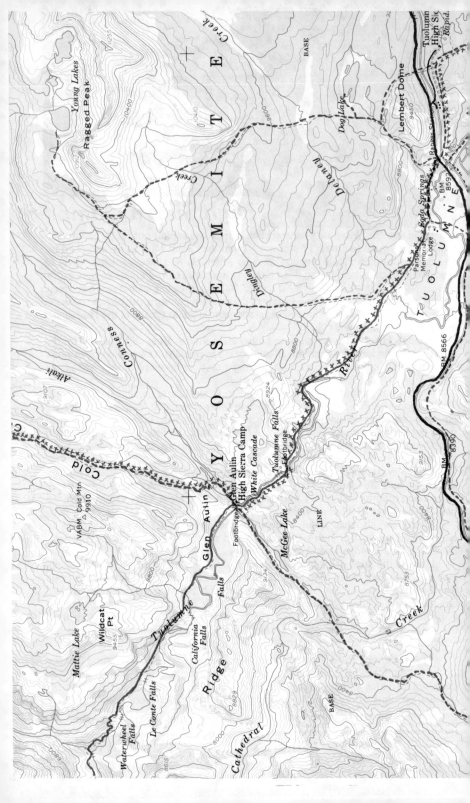

McGEE LAKE

The trail between Glen Aulin and May Lake provides a varied, easy day's trip. There is a short climb up to McGee Lake, followed by a generally level or easy grade for a couple of miles. The last section of the trail is a steady pull up to May Lake.

May Lake High Sierra Camp is beneath the eastern wall of Mt. Hoffman, on the shores of beautiful May Lake.

A side trip into the Ten Lakes basin will provide an abundance of scenery and fishing. Cross-country trips around the shoulders of Tuolumne Peak and also Mt. Hoffman are moderate in difficulty and give vast, panoramic views down into deep stream basins, and across to the east and north skyline crests of the Park boundary.

GLEN AULIN - MAY LAKE: - 8.4

Except for when you are resting on a rock near the trail you will be going downhill or uphill all day. It is a well developed trail from May Lake that goes down easy switchbacks for about a mile, then follows the old Tioga Pass dirt road, crossing the Tioga Pass highway at the lower end of Tenaya Lake. Then the trail follows the Forsyth Pass trail up the shoulder of Tenaya Creek about 2.5 miles to a junction with the Sunrise Lakes Trail. The Forsyth Pass trail connecting Tenaya Lake and Little Yosemite is an east trip, most of which runs through forest country.

79

The Sunrise High Sierra Camp is located on a small benchland just above beautiful Long Meadow. Views from here include the majestic peaks and crests of the northern end of the Cathedral Range.

Leaving Sunrise Camp the route goes north about a mile along a small section of the famous John Muir Trail to the Echo Creek Trail. From there it descends rapidly along the tumbling waters of Echo Creek, and its Cathedral Fork, to Echo Valley. There are short switchbacks up near the Merced River, to the lower end of Merced Lake. The High Sierra Camp is located at the upper end of the lake.

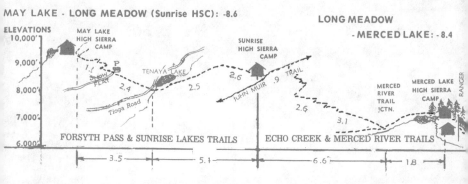

MAY LAKE - LONG MEADOW (Sunrise HSC): -8.6

LONG MEADOW
- MERCED LAKE: -8.4

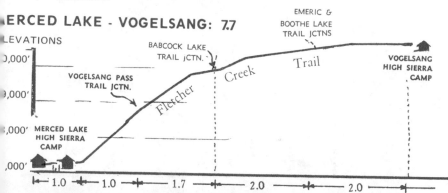

MERCED LAKE-VOGELSANG

The choice of routes depends upon the whim of each individual. The Fletcher Creek Trail is marked by a succession of plunging cascades and open meadows beneath towering canyon walls and rugged peaks. Side trips to Babcock and Emeric lakes afford good fishing and camping. The Vogelsang Pass Trail, following along the floor of Lewis Creek canyon, crosses the 10,700-foot crest at Vogelsang Pass, providing breathtaking views of a vast panorama of Mount Conness on the north, Lyell crest to the east and upper Merced River canyon to the south and west. A visit to this pass at daybreak, at sunset, or by moonlight is a never-to-be-forgotten adventure.

ERCED LAKE - VOGELSANG: 7.7

ELEVATIONS

EMERIC & BOOTHE LAKE TRAIL JCTNS

BABCOCK LAKE TRAIL JCTN.

VOGELSANG PASS TRAIL JCTN.

VOGELSANG HIGH SIERRA CAMP

MERCED LAKE HIGH SIERRA CAMP

Fletcher Creek Trail

0,000'
9,000'
,000'
,000'

|← 1.0 →|← 1.0 →|← 1.7 →|← 2.0 →|← 2.0 →|

81

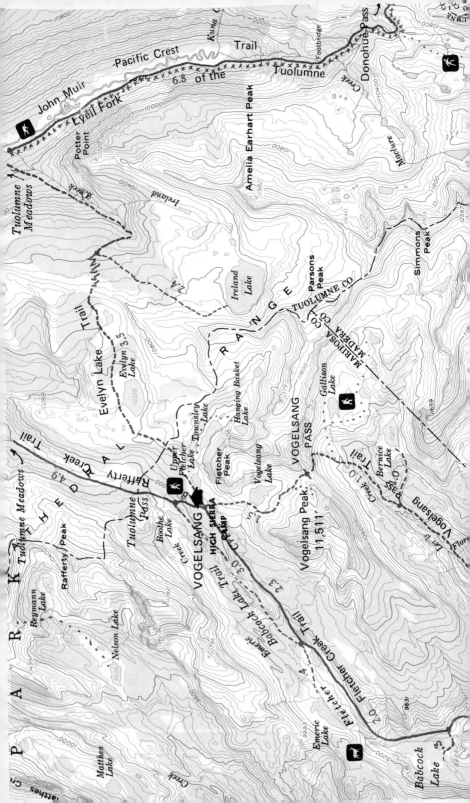

VOGELSANG-TUOLUMNE MEADOWS

ALPINE WILLOW

The Vogelsang Pass country is the highest in elevation on the loop trip connecting the High Sierra camps. It includes an unusual scenic area of rugged peaks as well as a score of lakes to entice the fisherman.

The shortest, more direct route is along Rafferty Creek. This trail follows along open high meadow areas to the brow of the Lyell Fork canyon where it drops by switchbacks to the junction with the John Muir Trail. From there it is about 1.5 miles to the main campground and activity center that includes the store, gas station, and Ranger Check Station.

To Tuolumne Meadows the Evelyn Lake Trail is varied and interesting. It includes Evelyn and Ireland lakes and follows down the level Lyell Fork Canyon. The shores of Ireland Lake were a meeting place of Yosemite and Mono Indians to trade acorns and obsidian.

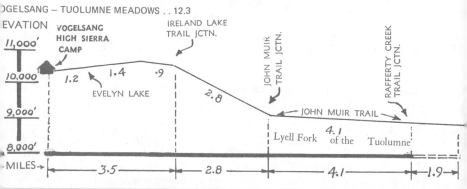

VOGELSANG – TUOLUMNE MEADOWS . . 12.3

VOGELSANG

83

NORTH COUNTRY

Old timers always referred to the untrailed wilderness above the Grand Canyon of the Tuolumne as the "North Country". In turn, it had discouraged the '49ers, emigrants, and timber cruisers. Gold, open land, and deep forests were not to be found in this glacier-scarred basin. Only a few foothill ranchers worked their flocks of sheep and beef cattle over into the lower Hetch Hetchy Valley and Jack Main Canyon. Even after it became a part of Yosemite National Park the area remained relatively unvisited.

Earliest trails marked out by the Army Cavalry units who patrolled the new Park followed the old Indian routes into and across the Sierra. Few, if any, signs were posted. In appropriate places "T" blazes were cut on trees and monuments stacked on open barren crossings. There were no native fish in any of the streams above the high falls to attract early fishermen. Later, wonderous tales came down out of the mountains as early "John Muirs" and "Norman Clydes" brought back stories to be told around the campfires at Tuolumne and Yosemite Valley.

Routes were soon pioneered down the Tuolumne Gorge to explore the magnificent "waterwheels" and the awesome canyon below them. From the west they pushed up the Tuolumne Canyon to the beautiful Rodgers and Benson lake area. Mountaineering groups soon set up camps in the high country and began exploring the peaks and crests along the headwaters of the Tuolumne. Trails were developed, signs set up at critical junctions to reassure those new to the mountains. Park Rangers were assigned to patrol duty "to save the wilderness from so many visitors and save the visitors from themselves" as one old-time Ranger put it.

The very ruggedness and isolation of the North Country has discouraged man's improvements. It has remained pretty much a natural environment with the exception of Hetch Hetchy and Tuolumne Meadows. The first was destroyed by the San Francisco Water Department, the other by road development along the route to the Great Sierra Consolidated Mining Company activity near Tioga Pass. Neither will ever regain its wilderness aspect. Today's visitors can never appreciate the full extent of their loss—they never saw it when herds of deer roamed the meadows, the song of birds at daylight presented an overwhelming rapture, and broad flower-decked meadows were unscarred by over-abundant trails.

Fortunately, there is a spreading awareness of the need to reduce man's impact on the high country. Realistic guideliness and practices are being adopted to repair some of the damage already done and slow the rate and extent of man's intrusion into the North Country.

BACKPACKING IN THE NORTH COUNTRY   EUGENE ROSE

Backpackers setting out into the North Country will find it a real wilderness experience. Of all regions in the Park, this is the least visited and those who do go, find an isolation from others in the many canyons and basins.

Trips should be planned with care. It is a big country taking a lot of time to explore. Once entering it you will be strictly on your own. Select your supplies carefully and plan your days well. Always allow a little extra time as a safety measure.

Your Wilderness Permit should faithfully reflect just where you plan to go and when you expect to return. Do not travel alone or cross-country unless it is really necessary. Eliminate all canned goods as much as possible. Use dried or dehydrated foods. Wood is usually available for small cook fires below 9600 feet. No longer can we "live off the country" in this sparse land, either for fish or fuel without the risk of despoiling it. The soil is thin and the winters are all too long and cold to recover much from even a small amount of over use.

Although people are sometimes few and far between, even animals are less numerous than in the forests of the Wawona country, you will have lots of company —mosquitoes. They will be around wherever you go except on high windy places and during the cool, crisp nights. A good insect repellent is an absolute must. BEWARE OF BEAR! They are much too eager to share your pack here!

Clothing should be selected with respect to warm days and cool nights. Changes in socks and shoes are as important as a little extra food. Select all your items with respect to bulk and weight. As an old timer put it: "count and weigh every item you take, then leave half of that at home, when you set out for a back country journey."

Camping facilities, lodge accommodations, supplies and stock-pack stations are available at most points of departure. Reservations are advised and made well in advance to avoid disappointment if you plan to use these facilities during the summer season.

There are no camping facilities near Hetch Hetchy. Plan to stay at Mather or allow enough time to make it to Beehive or Smith Meadow area at nightfall. Beehive is about a three hour journey from the dam and makes an ideal first night camp. There are good camping sites, supplies, and a pack station at the White Wolf Lodge and Tuolumne Meadows.

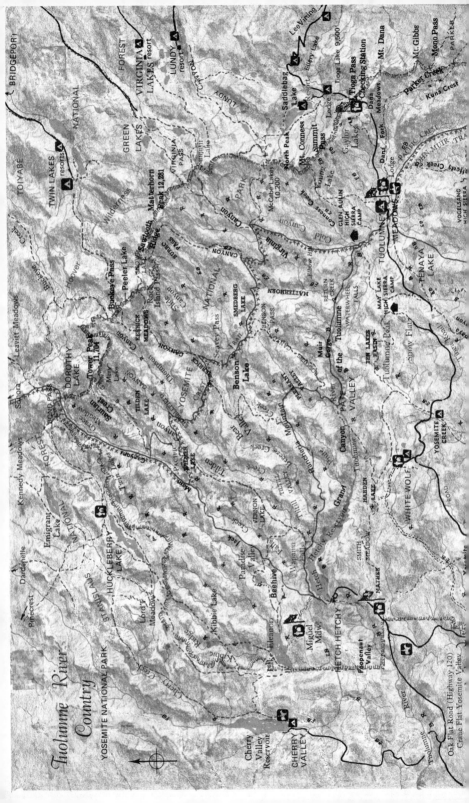

NORTH COUNTRY TRAILS

Within the Park the principal trailheads into the backcountry are located at Hetch Hetchy, White Wolf, and Tuolumne Meadows. West and north entries are located at Cherry Lake, Pinecrest, and Kennedy Meadows. Eastside trailheads are at Saddlebag/Lundy, Virginia Lakes, Green Lakes, Twin Lakes, and Leavitt Meadows. Three main routes cross the upper Tuolumne River basin:

A. PACIFIC CREST TRAIL (55 miles)
(Tuolumne Meadows to Dorothy Lake Pass)
Via Glen Aulin, Benson Lake, Tilden Lake, and upper Jack Main Canyon. This provides complete access to the western slope of the Sierra Crest between Mt. Conness and Tower Peak. An alternate high experience route in very rough country includes upper Matterhorn Canyon, Burro and Rock Island passes, and Kerrick Canyon.

B. GRAND CANYON OF THE TUOLUMNE (50 miles)
(Tuolumne Meadows - Hetch Hetchy)
Highlights include Pate Valley, Muir Gorge, Waterwheel Falls. Along the Rancheria Mountain section are three good trails leading into the high country:
Rodgers Canyon, Neall and Rodgers lakes, and Benson Lake.
Pleasant Valley, Bear Valley route to Kerrick Canyon.
Tiltill-Tilden Lake route. Includes access to many lakes. Largest and most scenic are Tilden and Mary lakes. (This is a good route in early summer when most of the canyons are flooded from spring runoff.)

C. JACK MAIN CANYON (25 miles)
(Hetch Hetchy to Bond/Dorothy Lake passes)
Includes Moraine Ridge, Paradise Valley, Wilmer Lake and Grace Meadows. Between Jack Main and the Tiltill-Tilden Lake Trail are located many unusual scenic spots and fishing lakes. Plenty of bear along the Moraine Ridge stretch and below Wilmer Lake. (This canyon is subject to flooding in early season—many mosquitoes!)

JACK MAIN CANYON

TUOLUMNE MEADOWS—MATTERHORN CANYON

The route of the Pacific Crest Trail between Tuolumne Meadows and Glen Aulin is an easy down grade along the Tuolumne River.

There is a good overnight camp there and plenty of bears. A side trip down to the Waterwheel Falls is a must, if you are going north. Allow at least a half day for the round trip. It is only a short two miles down switchbacks along the river, but it seems more like five miles back up the steep trail, especially on a hot, summer day. Let your eyes, not your feet, do the exploring along the glacial-polished apron next to the plunging torrent!

East of Glen Aulin, the route makes an easy climb up to Elbow Hill. Scattered pine and red fir are separated by small meadows to lend their charm in what is becoming more and more a rockbound country. Fishermen are well rewarded at McCabe Lakes and several of the higher lakes off Virginia Canyon.

Lower Matterhorn Canyon lies in a deep, forested valley. In spring the high waters at the stream crossing can present a problem to those with heavy packs. About a mile up canyon it opens up with rock-dotted meadows and splendid views of the Matterhorn Crest.

Most climbers make their ascents of the Matterhorn-Sawtooth Ridge from this area. The route including Mule Pass, Snow Lake, and Rock Island Pass is most rewarding in its alpine scenery and panorama views west across the Tuolumne Country and eastward down Robinson Creek-Twin Lakes area.

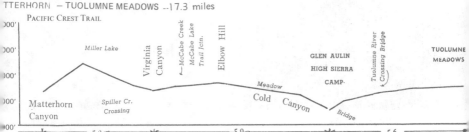

MATTERHORN — TUOLUMNE MEADOWS --17.3 miles

MATTERHORN CANYON   NPS PHOTO

NORTH FROM SHEPHERD CREST   ROCKY ROCKWELL

SHEPHERD CREST

Examples of great changes in the Sierra landscape abound in the Tuolumne headwaters basin. Not so evident are places that escaped the devastation of overriding glaciers, massive faulting, and erosion. Between the Matterhorn Crest and Mt. Whitney several of these ancient landscapes have survived. Flat, or gentle sloping summits tell their unique story—clues to the scene of pre-glacial times. They are found in such places as: Table Mountain and Diamond Mesa in the upper Kern River Canyon, at Dana Plateau and Shepherd Crest near the east boundary of Yosemite.

Lying on a flat-topped arm of the Sierra, it towers above upper Virginia Canyon. When observed from surrounding lowlands it gives the impression of being an erratic arm of the Sierra Crest and possessing a single craggy profile. Explorations have shown it to be actually two parallel crests enclosing the remnants of the *floor* of the ancient valley. Presumably, higher grounds rose on each side of a ravine until they were carried away by glacial activity.

In general, it is triangular in shape with its broadest, lowest side just above the 11,500' contour. Its highest edge lies to the north at the elevation of 11,860'. It is less than one-half mile in width and three-quarters of a mile long. The floor of nearby Virginia Canyon once carried a glacier 2000' thick and fourteen miles long that did not override this area.

90

Dana Crest: Looking south over Tioga-Lee Vining Canyon, Dana plateau, the east escarpment, and Owens Valley.

To quote from Francois Matthes's Geological Survey Report: Its isolated position amidst the titanic environment of craggy peaks and profound canyons is almost dramatically revealed. It seems like a little secluded skyland realm cut off from the fierce world around it by impregnable cliffs. Of all the ancient summit-tracts in the High Sierra, certainly the little valley on Shepherd Crest seems most remarkable. To a student of the Sierra it seems particularly precious because its non-glaciation … (confirms the same) … of many of the lofty tabular summits of the Sierra Nevada."

Only in recent years have geologists and general mountaineers developed an awareness of the full meaning and extent of such fragments of the Sierra's ancient landscape. Standing aloof from glacial impact, wildlife activity, and human intrusion, it has survived undisturbed through the ages and is fittingly referred to by Matthes as

"The Little Lost Valley on Shepherd Crest."

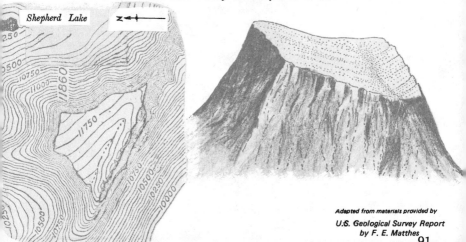

Adapted from materials provided by

U.S. Geological Survey Report
by F. E. Matthes

91

EASTERN SIERRA APPROACHES
(Tioga Pass-Virginia Pass)

Campgrounds near Tioga Lake junction and at Saddlebag Lake provide ideal settings in the Hoover Wilderness while getting acclimated to the rarified atmosphere. Hikers to Gardinsky Lake, Oneida Lake, and Warren Canyon will find them most rewarding in fish and scenery. The whole area east of Mt. Conness lies in a sub-alpine setting, with many well-stocked lakes and streams. Prize catches have been taken at Saddlebag. The shortest route to climbing Mt. Conness or visiting its glacier is made from near Alpine Lake.

History Buffs will find interest in the ghost town and mill site of the Old May Lundy Mine up in Lundy Canyon or at Bennettville, about a mile from the Tioga Lodge. Evidences can be found of the Great Sierra Consolidated Mining Company where a dream of silver brought no gold!

In Lundy Canyon is a resort with store and campgrounds. Good fishing is found in Lundy Lake or Creek and in the upper headwaters basin at the foot of the range near North and Conness peaks.

The eastern entry to the Pacific Crest Trail at Virginia Canyon can be reached by either Virginia Pass (10,500') or Summit Lake Pass (10,200'). More than a half-dozen lakes provide good fishing at Virginia Lakes (9700') which is about seven miles west of Conway Summit on Hwy. 395. There is a good campground and limited supplies at the resort lodge. Upper Green Creek Canyon offers excellent fishing at Green, West, and East Lakes.

From Green Lake (8880') the trail most used lies south to East Lake and Summit Lake Pass. The route via Virginia Pass has been improved by the Forest Service and provides a good crossing. Conditions from Virginia Pass to the Burro Pass-Matterhorn Peak area vary with the seasons and should be checked out before considering cross-countrying. Camiaca Peak (11,739') is a Class 2 climb from Summit Lake.

LUNDY CANYON   ROCKY ROCKWELL

MATTERHORN CANYON   NPS PHOTO

MATTERHORN-KERRICK CANYONS

Here, in the very upper benches at the bend of Matterhorn Canyon the backpacker will find the ultimate in seclusion and scenic grandeur of the Northern Sierra.

The many lakes, flowers, and forests in this region; the typical High Sierra atmosphere; the meandering stream of Matterhorn Canyon creek, and the remoteness of these canyons make this a backpacker's paradise. It is an ideal layover spot. The towering crags of Sawtooth Ridge and the Matterhorn Crest invite exploration and photography.

Some years there is a large snowfield across the slope between the Mule Pass and Snow Lake so care should be taken. In fact, most all of these canyons are comparatively deep and narrow with shaded north slopes where snow remains until well into the summer.

Hikers in the backcountry travelling the heads of these canyons along the Park boundary having need of short emergency exits from the Park will find the passes and trails along the eastern boundary relatively easy to traverse. Although some are in rough condition, they do provide contact with a number of points on the east side that can be reached within a day.

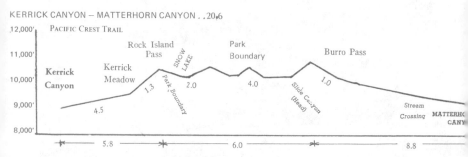

KERRICK CANYON — MATTERHORN CANYON . . 20.6

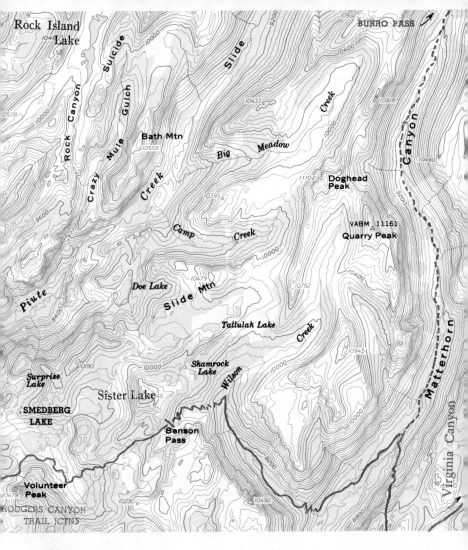

SMEDBERG-ROCK ISLAND WILDERNESS

Between Smedberg Lake and Rock Island Lake the upper Piute Creek Basin includes a wilderness visited only by venturesome backpackers. Its abrupt, glacier-slick slopes have discouraged horses and trail building. Its sparse forest cover of lodgepole, hemlock and whitebark pine requires the use of fuel stoves. (All this area is above 9500' level—no wood fires.)

Smedberg Lake has been a favorite to those seeking a remote High Sierra experience. Almost alpine in character the pocket meadows are a wonder of wild flowers in early summer. Its neighboring lakes, Surprise and Sister offer a variety of settings. The low, saddle invites exploration of Shamrock, Doe and Tallulah lakes.

Neall and Rodgers lakes are of similar elevation with towering craggy peaks and are only a short distance to the west.

BENSON LAKE

Benson Lake lies at the crossroads of the northern Yosemite Sierra. Entry is made by several routes, all of which offer a great variety of scenery, fishing, and all around good camping. Both its beauty and proximity to many other unusual scenic areas make it a most desirable stop where a base camp can be made for exploration nearby. The floor of the valley above the half-mile long lake is quite level, heavily wooded, and sheltered between towering granite walls.

In the early season the streams are turbulent and high. Best time and conditions for hiking in this part of Yosemite are in the middle of July when the water is down, the weather is milder, and most of the mosquitoes are gone.

Those going into the upper canyon basins by way of Rodgers Canyon will be well rewarded by the inclusion of Neall Lake and Rodgers Lake. Without a doubt these are two of the finest gems of the North Country. Whole sections of the trail are magnificent "rock gardens" of sub-alpine and alpine flowers.

NEALL LAKE

Leavitt Meadow Dorothy Lake

This newly completed section of the Pacific Crest Trail follows on a more remote route than its previous one along the West Walker River. Its upper part includes a half dozen small lakes along Cascade Creek, Cinko Lake, the Long Lakes, Chain of Lakes, and upper Kennedy Canyon. Between there and the rim above Leavitt Lake it parallels the 10,000' crest where panoramic views of the basins to the east and north are most rewarding. There is a 3.5 mile unimproved road between the trailhead on the Sonora Pass Road and the Leavitt Lake. (No established campsites at the lake, and very little firewood.)

This section of the Pacific Crest Trail between Sonora Pass Road and the head of the West Walker River at Dorothy Lake Pass, presents an exciting venture to southbound traverers headed for Benson Lake, Matterhorn Canyon, and Tuolumne Meadows.

DOROTHY LAKE — SONORA PASS ROAD
(via Cinco Lake, Chain Lakes, Hollywood Basin. Leavitt Lake)

ELEVATIONS		
PACIFIC CREST TRAIL ××××××××	. 14.5	
West Walker River Trail ———	. 13.5	

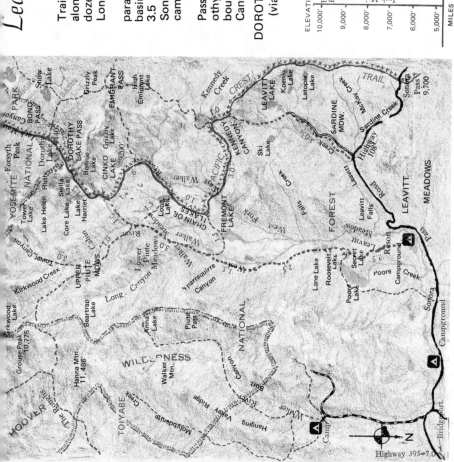

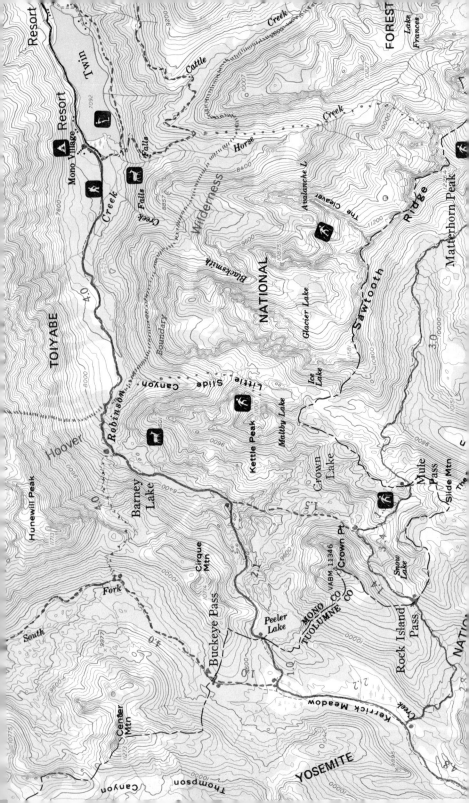

EASTERN APPROACHES TO SAWTOOTH CREST & MATTERHORN

From Twin Lakes the eastern face of the Sierra escarpment presents a most formidable confrontation along the base of the Sawtooth Ridge. Boat-fishermen on Upper Twin and RV campers in extensive campgrounds along Robinson Creek and the lakes are content to enjoy the magnificence of these peaks by just looking as eager climbers arrive daily and make plans for ascents. Climber's guides indicate Class 2 ascents from Burro Pass and from the vicinity of Horse Creek Pass.

Actually the routes up Horse Creek and Blacksmith Creek are used primarily only by the more experienced climbers. The most popular route is by way of Barney and Crown lakes and then cross-country to just north of Slide Mountain. The popularity of this country with climbers and general backpackers is attested by the Wilderness Permit reports showing more than 8,000 "visitor night use". Most of these are, of course, during August.

Changing seasons present changing conditions. Climbers can approach the area via Little Slide Canyon with routes ranging in difficulty from a steep scramble to Class 5.8 requiring special equipment and skills. For the less adventuresome, visits to the basins below the glaciated rampart are adequate. Fishing is good in some of the half-dozen lakes such as Barney, Maltby, and Crown. Note: Twin Lakes lies some twelve miles west of Bridgeport. Services include two resorts, campgrounds, stores, boat rentals, and a trailer park.

MATTERHORN & SAWTOOTH RIDGE   RUSSELL JOHNSON

GRAND CANYON OF THE TUOLUMNE

The trip down through the Grand Canyon of the Tuolumne affords a never-to-be-forgotten experience. One's personal involvement and exposure to a landscape carved out of the bedrock of the earth by the momentous forces of nature is unique. From its beginnings in glacial ponds and snowpacked slopes of majestic peaks to the shimmering Hetch Hetchy Reservoir, it is the unfolding story of a great river.

The tremendous gorge and its headwater tributaries tell the story of the largest of the ancient Sierra glaciers. The Yosemite High Sierra has been referred to as a living textbook of geology. It might well be added that its summary chapter is written here, where ice and running water have wrought their inevitable changes in the ancient Sierra landscape. The extensive peaceful, flowered meadows at Tuolumne and Dana are the entry prelude to the tumultuous lower canyon to the west. The quiet and restful walks through the meadows give way near Glen Aulin to an increased venture with raging torrents, leaping cascades and unbelievable sheer canyon walls.

GLEN AULIN is a small aspen flat located a short distance below the High Sierra Camp. Pines, alders, willows and pocket meadows provide a favorable camping place.

Between Glen Aulin and Return Creek the river puts on its grandest display. Deep cuts into the streambed deflect the full force of the river into great arcs or *waterwheels*. In late afternoon the sweeping mantles of spray are transformed into multicolored rainbow clouds.

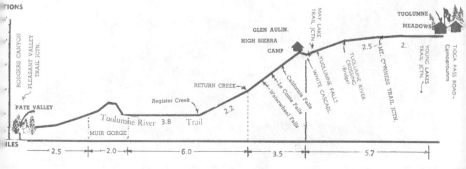

The deepest, most inaccessible part of the canyon lies in Muir Gorge. The trail literally hangs on the high north wall. Pause at the highest western point on the trail. Splendid view into the gorge below! From there can be visualized the ancient Tuolumne Ice Field.

Reflect on its magnitude, almost a mile deep in the canyon before you extending west, north and east to the horizon peaks. Too tall to be overridden and too massive to be plucked asunder in their time, these stalwart peaks stood like ghostly sentinels above the spreading ice fields as it filled to overflowing. Its excess spilled over into the upper Merced and Tenaya canyons, past the crags of the Cathedral and Chief Tenaya peaks. To the east it flowed over the Sierra crest at Donohue, Mono, Parker, and Tioga passes and carved out the steep canyons along the eastern edge of the escarpment. Today's terminal moraines mark the limits of their flow below the glacial tarn lakes they left in their passing. The crests of these surviving peaks provide us with clues as to the nature of the ancient, pre-glacial landscape. It is believed to have been a thousand feet higher than the present crests and the erosive forces of nature carried it away down into the great Central Valley to the west.

MUIR GORGE   NPS PHOTO

PATE VALLEY

Once the summer home of the Miwok people, it is now a junction trailhead to routes leading north, east and west. Here the Tuolumne River is peaceful and sublime before it plunges into the narrow gorge leading west to Hetch Hetchy Reservoir. Numerous pictographs are found along the north edge of the meadow and oak flat. It is warm and dry and well populated with rodents. (Note: Pate Valley has been well known for its ample supply of rattlesnakes—so beware!)

PATE VALLEY   NPS PHOTO

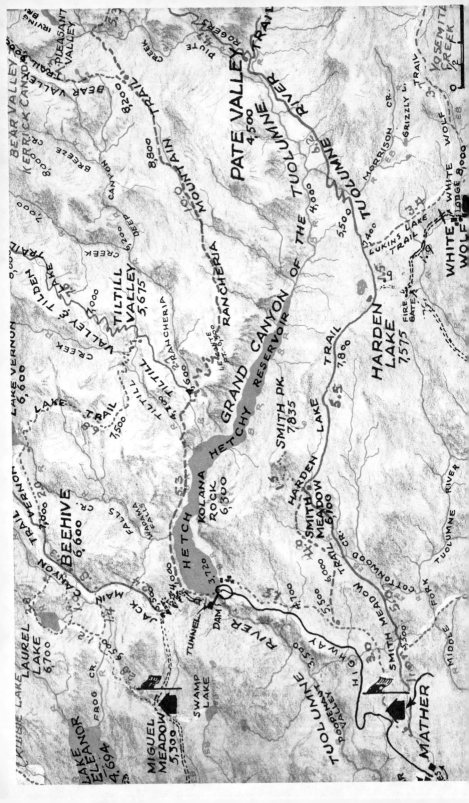

HETCH HETCHY/MATHER-PATE VALLEY

Entry into the west end of Pate Valley can be made at Mather-Hetch Hetchy or White Wolf-Harden Lake trailheads. Backpackers have a choice of two interesting routes.

RANCHERIA MOUNTAIN TRAIL follows along the north shore of Hetch Hetchy Reservoir. It is a good early season entry when higher trailheads may still be under snow. Generally, it is warm and dry along the latter part of the season. There, is the most intimate views of shining water and sheer granite walls of the lower Grand Canyon of the Tuolumne. Although the trail is higher in elevation, it is moderate in difficulty with a few steep, rough stretches between Rancheria Creek and the top of the mountain.

Pleasant Valley and neighboring lakes are all their names imply. This is the best route to trailheads to the Tiltill-Tilden Lake Trail, Bear Valley and Kerrick Canyons, and the Rodgers Canyon-Smedberg-Benson Lake area. Their secluded, seldom visited streams and lakes provide good fishing and excellent camping.

Services at Mather include bus, accommodations, store with supplies, horses and camping. At Hetch Hetchy there are no services or campgrounds.

SMITH MEADOW TRAIL out of Mather includes several long meadows and the most heavily forested region in the North Country. A side trip to Smith Peaks is most rewarding for the magnificent views over the lower Tuolumne Basin. By starting at White Wolf-Harden Lake a day's hiking is saved when going to Pate Valley or beyond as this is the shortest and most direct route. This was the old moccasin tracks trail of the Miwok people.

Services at White Wolf include campgrounds, lodge and limited supplies. Harden Lake is close to the brim of the Tuolumne Canyon. There is good fishing early in the season.

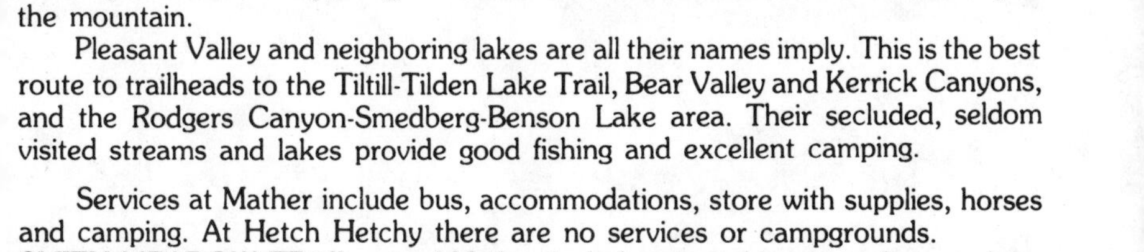

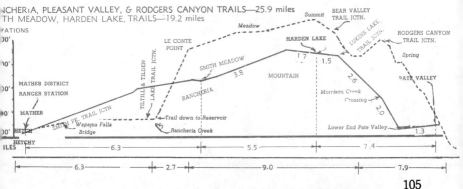

EAST FLANGE ROCK 9,909

LOWER RELIEF VALLEY 8,223

RELIEF RESV. 7,500

SUMMIT

SAUCER MDW.

RELIEF PEAK 10,788

KENNEDY L. 7,820

KENNEDY PEAK 10,677

COOPER MDW. 8,300

UPPER RELIEF VALLEY 8,900

8000

RELIEF CREEK 8,500

SHEEP CAMP 6.0

SONORA CANYON

LEWIS LAKES 9,250

LUNCH MDW. 9,800

VALLEY

BROWN BEAR PASS 9,700

EMIGRANT BASIN

HWY. 108 LEAVITT MEAD

BOUND

GRANITE DOME 10,300

EMIGRANT BASIN

SPRING MDW.

BLACKHAWK MTN. 10,327

EMIGRANT MEADOW LAKE 9,400

TRAIL

STANISLAUS NATIONAL FOREST

GRIZZLY PK 10,250

LAKE VALLEY 8,900

STARVATION LAKE

SUMMIT L.

LONG L. 8,750

EMIGRANT LAKE 8,850

9,000

SUMMIT L.

BOND

EMIGRANT BASIN BOUNDARY

PIUTE MDW. 8,200

PIUTE L. 8,900

DEER L. 8,400

BUCK LAKES 7,850

9,600

HELEN LAKE

HORSE MDW.

BIGLOW

BLACK MEADOW 9,000

LOUISE CANYON

BOURLAND MDW. TRAIL

BUCK MDW.

WOOD L. 7,825

COW MDW. 7,800

PARK

BOUNDARY 8,350

BIGLOW 10,510

BIGLOW PK

CHITTENDEN PEAK 10,135

KE PK.

10,000

HYATT LAKE 7,918

GILETT MTN. 8,300

HUCKLEBERRY LAKE 7,750

NORTH FK.

LAKES 8,850

TWIN

KENDRICK PK 10,346

FAWN L. 8,100

HAYSTACK PK 9,966

PCT

MAIN 8,566

JACK

8000

TIL LAK 88

CHERRY CR.

LORDS MEADOW 7,700

EAST FK.

CHERRY

NATIONAL

RICHARDSON PK 9,845

BEAR L.

SCHOFIELD PK 9,913

RIDGE

CHERRY CANYON

YOSEMITE

BOUNDARY RIDGE TRAIL

KIBBIE CR.

MANY ISL. L.

BOUNDARY L.

SPOTTED FAWN L.

INFERNO L.

BIG ISL. L.

HOUR GLASS LAKES

WILMER LAKE 7,800

XXX RIDGE

COMB RIDGE

KIBBIE CR.

KIBBIE LAKE 6,385

CREEK

BEARUP L. 7,500

PARADISE VALLEY

1.8

BAILEY

3.0

STUBBLEFIELD CANYON

FLORA L. 6,800

KENDERICK CANYON

EDITH L. 6,603

MINER L.

ARDITH L. 7,500

ANDREWS PK 8,500

2.3

TILDEN CANYON

6,500

2.0

TILDEN CREEK

LAKE ELEANOR HETCH HETCHY

BARTLETT

FROG CR.

BRANNIGAN 7,300 LAKES

RANCHERIA

LAUREL

ELEANOR CR.

JACK MAIN CANYON TRAIL

VERNON CREEK

MORAINE

VERNON LAKE 6,600

MT. GIBSON 8,400

TILTILL LAKE TRAIL

VALLEY

1.8

LAKE ELEANOR 4,094

BEEHIVE 6,600

FALLS

TILTILL TRAIL

TILTILL CR.

STILTILL VALLEY 5,675

DEEP CANYON

PLEASANT E BEAR

MIGUEL MEADOW 5,200

WAPAMA FALL

BRIDGE

TILTILL

MOUNTAIN TRAIL

HETCH HETCHY

TUNNEL

DAM 4000

KOLANA ROCK

GRAND CANYON OF THE TUOLUMNE R.

HETCH HETCHY RES.

RANCHERIA LE CONTE POINT 6,500

YOSEMITE VALLEY

JACK MAIN CANYON

This canyon carries the waters of Falls Creek that extends northeast to the Park boundary at Bond Pass and includes a large number of small lakes as well as Vernon, Branigan, Wilmer, Tilden, Mary, and Dorothy lakes. If you enjoy a back-country of medium elevation (6000'-8000') where the summers are pleasantly warm, the trails are of easy grade, and you never run out of lakes to visit, then this is the place. Cross-country day and overnight jaunts from a base camp are especially easy. Low, rounded ridges and saddles between canyons invite a continuous sequence of answers to the question: "Well, where will we go today!"

Good camp areas are found at Beehive, Paradise Valley, Lake Vernon, Branigan Lakes, and Wilmer. Any trip into this country should include Tilden Lake and upper Tilden Canyon to Mary Lake. This is a *wilderness* type area where trails and signboards have never been developed.

Just over the northern crest lies the famous Emigrant Basin. Best entries are at Cherry Creek, Lord's Meadow, and at Huckleberry Lake. The Huckleberry Lake-Jack Main Canyon area is most popular with backpackers out of Pinecrest, Kennedy and Leavitt meadows. (Old maps indicating cross-country travel between Twin Lakes and upper Jack Main to Grace Meadows invite problems. This country is very rough. Better go around by Horse Meadow and Bond Pass.)

TILDEN LAKE

MAIN CANYON— MATTERHORN CANYON . . .28.0

107

JACK MAIN CANYON TRAIL—14.5 miles

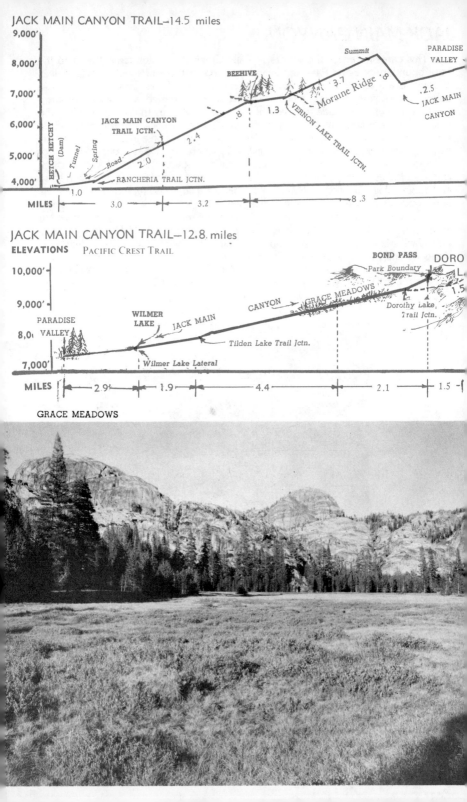

9,000'				Summit	PARADISE VALLEY
8,000'				Moraine Ridge .8	
7,000'		BEEHIVE		3.7	.2.5 JACK MAIN CANYON
6,000'	JACK MAIN CANYON TRAIL JCTN.	.8	1.3 VERNON LAKE TRAIL JCTN.		
5,000'	Spring 2.4 Road 2.0				
4,000'	HETCH HETCHY (Dam) Tunnel RANCHERIA TRAIL JCTN.				

MILES |— 1.0 —|— 3.0 —|— 3.2 —|— 8 .3 —|

JACK MAIN CANYON TRAIL—12.8. miles

ELEVATIONS   PACIFIC CREST TRAIL

				BOND PASS	DORO
10,000'			Park Boundary		L
9,000'		CANYON	GRACE MEADOWS		1.5
	WILMER LAKE JACK MAIN			Dorothy Lake Trail Jctn.	
8,00	PARADISE VALLEY	Tilden Lake Trail Jctn.			
7,000'	Wilmer Lake Lateral				

MILES |— 2.9 —|— 1.9 —|— 4.4 —|— 2.1 —|— 1.5 —|

GRACE MEADOWS

EMIGRANT BASIN-HOOVER WILDERNESS AREAS

The Hoover and Emigrant Basin Wilderness Areas lying adjacent to the Northern boundary of Yosemite National Park provide a mellow, intermediate experience that gives a pleasant contrast and relief to the busy multiple-use forests below them. With a quite different philosophy than either the National Forests or the National Park system they offer a unique place "where the earth and its community of life are untrammeled by man, where man himself is a visitor who does not remain."

Hoover Wilderness is characterized by its many U-shaped canyons. At their heads are remnants of five glaciers. Excelsior and Dunderberg, both exceeding 12,300', are its highest peaks. A good dozen others, especially along the Sawtooth Ridge, challenge beginners and experts. Its northern area includes a half-dozen popular trails leading west and south into the outback of Yosemite North Country.

Emigrant Basin includes more than 100,000 acres of unique wilderness. Lying north and west of Yosemite's boundary, it is an undulating plateau isolated by rough crests along its eastern and southern limits and, to the north and west by the abrupt 2000'-3000' drop-off into the Canyon of the Stanislaus. Of its more than a hundred granite shored lakes the largest are Huckleberry, Emigrant, Buck, Long, Hyatt, and Biglow. Its scattered forests include ponderosa, western white, and Jeffrey pine, as well as red and white fir, incense cedar and western juniper. Scattered groves of lodgepole and whitebark pine are found on the northern slopes.

Trailheads and principal routes into the backcountry of both areas are shown on the map page 110. (Numbers match those on the map)

NORTH COUNTRY AND WILDERNESS ENTRANCE POINTS

Most of the trails into the northern Yosemite and its adjacent Wilderness areas were determined by the passage of game and Indians in their seasonal migrations between the foothills and the high country feeding grounds. Later stockmen followed these routes to high mountain grasslands. Today's trails have been kept to a minimum. The region is ideally suited to a backpacker's desire to cross-country travel as there has been a limited amount of man's improvements. Its many entry points make available almost a thousand square miles of wilderness.

WESTERN ENTRY

(1) HETCH HETCHY or MATHER: Trails lead to Jack Main Canyon, Benson Lake and Tuolumne Meadows. (Parking lot near the dam, but NO camping here.) The nearest camps are at Middle Fork and Carlan. Supplies and stock are available at Evergreen and Mather.

(25) CHAIN LAKES: The Bourland Meadow Road is a long trip in from the Clavey Meadows and Big Oak Flat Road. No services available. Some five miles between roadend and Chain Lakes via Bourland Creek Trail. Usually good stream and lake fishing. It is only a mile from the lakes to a junction with the Pine Valley Trail. About three miles east of Grouse Lake make an exceptional fine loop trip that includes Hyatt, Pingree, Big, Yellowhammer and Leighton lakes.

(26) CHERRY LAKE: Shortest trail entry to western Jack Main Canyon and the Kibbie Ridge-Huckleberry Lake areas. One route is via Tuolumne City and Cottonwood Lake Road (I-No 4). Inquire at Groveland or Sonora Forest Service Ranger Station. The second route is to turn off Big Oak Flat Road (Hwy. 108) about six miles east of Groveland Ranger Station, near San Jose Camp, then twenty miles north. There is a hikers parking lot at the dam, campground, pay phone, pack station but NO stores or supplies. Wilderness Permits can be obtained ONLY at Groveland Ranger Station.

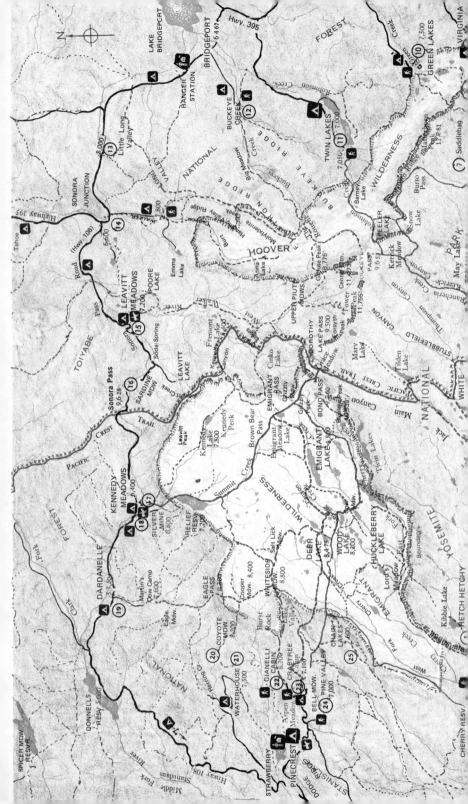

TIOGA ROAD ENTRY

(2) WHITE WOLF: Tuolumne River Trail leads to Pate Valley, Benson Lake, Matterhorn and Tuolumne Meadows.

(3) YOSEMITE CREEK: Trailhead north to Ten Lakes Basin and south to Yosemite Valley via Yosemite Creek. Campground is a few miles off Tioga Road on Yosemite Creek. No services at the bridge parking space.

(4) TENAYA LAKE: Trailhead: South of Yosemite and Merced Lake via Forsyth Pass Trail; east to Tuolumne Meadows and north to May Lake, Ten Lakes Basin, Glen Aulin and Virginia Canyon-Matterhorn Country. No services—a "walk-in" campground, picnic sites, parking area, and telephone.

(5) TUOLUMNE MEADOWS: Trailhead to all principal trails in Yosemite with multiple services, Park Naturalists programs and conducted field trips.

SONORA PASS ROAD

(12) BUCKEYE CREEK TRAIL: Trails lead to upper Kerrick Meadow via Buckeye Pass and to upper Piute Meadows and Upper Jack Main Canyon via Dorothy Lake Pass. There are no services, open area to camp at roadend, six miles west of Bridgeport Ranger Station.

(14) SONORA JUNCTION: Trails to Molybdinite Creek and Upper Burt Canyon in the northern Hoover Wilderness Area. Campgrounds: Chris Flat—3 miles N; Opal Obsidian—3 miles S on Little Walker River; and Sonora Bridge—2 miles W. No services.

(15) LEAVITT MEADOW (7700'): Trails up West Walker River to Upper Piute Meadows, Upper Jack Main Canyon via Dorothy Lake Pass, and Emigrant Wilderness via Emigrant Pass. Services include lodge, supplies, campground, and pack station.

(16) SONORA PASS (9628'): Pacific Crest Trail crossing north to Tahoe etc.

(17 & 18) KENNEDY MEADOWS (6400'): Trails south to all parts of the Emigrant Wilderness and North Country of Yosemite. Services include lodge, campgrounds, supplies and stock.
Silver Mine Trailhead is little used. No services available.

(19) DARDENELLE (5750'): Trails into northern and western Emigrant Basin and northern Yosemite via Eagle Pass and Huckleberry Lake. There is a lodge, campground and Ranger Station.

(20-24) PINECREST (5621'): This is a most popular entry center to the Emigrant Basin and northern Yosemite. It is a complete summer and winter resort community with extensive facilities and services available. Trailheads out of Coyote Meadow (20), Waterhouse (21), are not used as frequently as those farther south at Gianelli (22), Crabtree (23), or Bell Meadow (24). BURRO PASS

Yosemite Environment

Over the short space of some 60-70 miles between the chapparel oak foothills and the Sierran crest, climatic and food types supporting bird and mammal life are as extensive as those resulting changing conditions that cover the wide range of western America lying between the southwestern deserts and northern Arctic tundra regions almost 2,000 miles to the north.

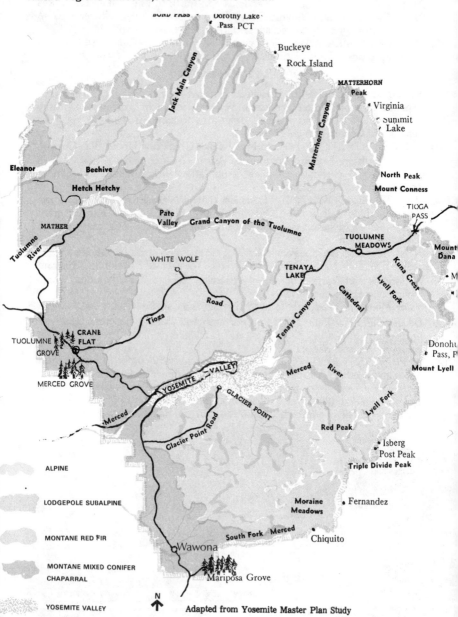

Adapted from Yosemite Master Plan Study

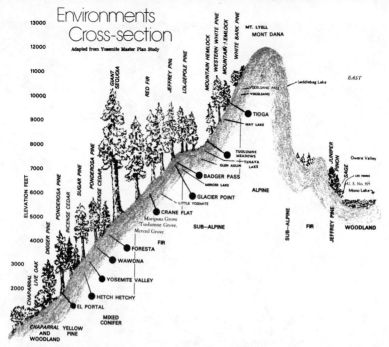

Environments Cross-section

Adapted from Yosemite Master Plan Study

No two, well established species occupy the same ecologic space; each has its own peculiar place for foraging and for making secure itself and its young. A general environment's amplitude determines the species and the quantity of those living there.

The natural interdependence of all living things in the backcountry is constant not only in relation to birds, insects, and animals, but also in the plant communities they inhabit. Nuthatches, creepers, woodpeckers, warblers, junkos, and chickadees earnestly seek out every nook and crevice for insects. Just as the forest provides them with food and shelter, they, in turn, provide the forest with their watchful gathering of insects that might be harmful. The giant ponderosa pine needs the smallest insect-seeking birds as much as they need the forest that shelters them. In its entirety, the wilderness residents blend like a well-rehearsed symphony where each secures its own moment of attention in nature's orchestration of the wild.

Actually, the life of the forest depends upon the natural death of some of its members. As some insects overcome trees their decaying pulp eventually becomes an important part of the forest floor for food and moisture where new, young trees can germinate. The loss of some becomes the advantages of others. Near Tuolumne Meadows, for example, a large number of former lodgepole pines have, over the years, been replaced by mountain hemlock.

Even fire, within limits, opens areas to sunlight and freshness to encourage the growth of new plants and improve the quality of those already there. With persistent, and at times frantic energy, man has sought to control every fire. As meadows become overgrown and matted, and as trees were allowed to crowd in great numbers, they were reduced to spindly stalks reaching to the sky for sunlight, weakened by too much competition.

The interaction of all living things in the Yosemite wilderness, including man's presence there, carries real responsibilities with respect to its preservation. In the higher zones where life at best is most fragile, the seasons are so short they permit only minimal replacement of any man-made damage.

113

MEADOW AND ROCK GARDENS

Washington Lily

SHOOTING STARS

Yosemite's western foothill valleys to her eastern rocky crests present an extreme range of soil and climatic conditions conducive to a multitude of wildflowers. Starting in the lower hills and moving upward over a period of several weeks, the visitor could live in a land of eternal spring until mid-summer when suddenly one night, fall arrives with cold nights and frosty morning meadows and it is time for the retreat to begin.

During this brief season of life, the flower garden of meadows, warm sandy slopes, and craggy ledges present themselves in almost breathless haste to complete their life-cycles before summer's end. With almost 1,500 kinds of flowering plants in the Park, no complete list is attempted here—only a few of those the writer found unusual pleasure in on his travels.

The high meadows near Crane Flat and along the Glacier Point road abound with shooting stars in early summer. In shady turns along a granite walled trail, a spring-fed rock garden may well include a mixture of monkey flower, mimulus, leopard lily, and columbine. Across sandy slopes the mountain phlox produces a mass of rose-purple to purple-tinted flowers close to the ground. Fortunate is the exploring hiker who, crossing the bushy slope of the North Rim, encounters a towering Washington lily, rising in elegant defiance of a rustic neighborhood with its pure white bloom heavy with fragrance.

DEER BRUSH

PUSSY PAWS

COLUMBINE

MONKEY FLOWER

Wildflower displays, like gold, are where you find them. However, in proper season, they will usually be found in the meadow areas at the lower end of the Valley floor, along the Tioga Road, near Wawona, and along the Glacier Point Road. Some of the better displays have been found at Crane Flat, Bridalveil and McGurk meadows, Empire Meadow, and the upper benches of Dana Fork at Tuolumne Meadows. Spring-in-summer displays will be found along the trails in Pleasant Valley, Rodgers Canyon, Upper Lyell Fork of the Merced, and the sunny slopes near Vogelsang Pass.

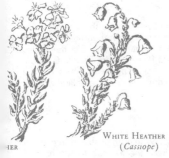

WHITE HEATHER
(Cassiope)

Reserved for the most hardy of mountaineers is the rock garden collection of plants that include the tiny alpine willow, the red and the white heather, and the sky-blue polemonium. Their perversity in growing in such unlikely places as 12,000 foot skyline ridges is matched by that of those who came just to look at them.

DOUGLAS PHLOX

BROADLEAVED TREES AND SHRUBS

Visitors to Yosemite are so impressed with the dark pines and firs that extend like a great green robe over the middle mountain elevations, they often overlook the less pretentious shrubs and broadleaved trees nearby. These, filling in the open spaces the evergreens have avoided, provide gaiety and color with their early season blossoms and late autumn leaves.

Identifying most trees can become less confusing by working out a simple rule-of-thumb guide based upon their location and general appearance. For example, in the Tuolumne Meadows area, practically all of the needle-bearing trees are lodgepole pines. In specially suited spots are a few junipers and mountain hemlocks. Above the Meadows, at treeline, are the whitebark pines. Willows and quaking aspen need lots of water and usually grow near streams and wet regions below talus slopes.

Now, with less than one-half dozen varieties of plants to learn, the visitor can let the rest of his visit become an extension of his curiosity and enjoyment by adding a few new ones. Discovering a new species is that day he finds one that is new to him such as an alpine willow or sky pilot. After general consideration to elevation, location of the immediate area, and appearance, soon you will become a self-acknowledged authority with a list that grows with your travels on Yosemite trails. Park Naturalists hold conducted walks and many inexpensive booklets are available for your assistance.

BLACK OAK

LIVE OAK

BIGLEAF MAPLE

WILLOW

ALPINE WILLOW

The most frequent broadleaved trees found along the Wawona Road, the Big Oak Flat Road, and on the Valley floor are:

THE GOLDEN CUP OAK (Canyon Live Oak) is evergreen, grows up to 50 feet; some reach ages of 500-600 years. The leaves are small and its acorns are set in shallow, yellow fuzz-coated cups.

THE CALIFORNIA BLACK OAK is the West's largest mountain oak. This is a deciduous tree with very dark bark. Leaves are large and put forth great color in the fall. Its rich brown deep-cup acorns were used by Indians as a main food supply (after grinding and leaching).

THE BIG-LEAF MAPLE, found in the lower, warm canyons where there is running water and good soil is a large, graceful tree with a gnarly trunk. On the Valley floor, along the Merced River and in Tenaya Canyon, they make a great color display in the fall. The seeds are set adrift in the wind in double pods resembling wings of a large insect.

The ever-present WILLOW in both bush and tree forms grows along streams from the foothills to the highest meadows. The slender, limber branches bearing narrow pale-green leaves shade the trout nearby and make nesting shelter for birds. ALPINE WILLOW grow beyond the last whitebark pine in moist snow-fed tundra sending forth its limbs in matted patterns just under the surface. It presents its bloom with tiny, 2-inch tall catkins with a few narrow, dark green leaves to protect and encourage its efforts in such a difficult place.

PACIFIC DOGWOOD (cornus nuttallii) The dogwood needs little direct sunlight as their photosynthesis process operates on much less sunlight than most broad-leaved trees. It grows to heights of 20-30 feet. Their slender, willowy trunk is covered by smooth grayish bark. The flowers are actually not the large white petal-like bracts but the small button-like cluster in the center.

Along the roads near Wawona, in Yosemite Valley, and at Crane Flat, the dogwood lives modestly in close association with the large pines and conifers seeking their shade during the warm summers and their protection from violent winter storms. In the autumn, with gaudy display, they present a blaze of reds, browns, yellows and golds. It is then the off-season tourist finds it is the "in season" to be in Yosemite.

Two trees that enjoy shade and plenty of water are the CALIFORNIA LAUREL (Oregon Myrtle, bay, and pepperwood) with its heavy, rich, aromatic leaves, and the WHITE ALDER with its pale gray bark and fruit that resembles a very small pine cone.

Many lower foothill residents prefering the day slopes include the BUCKEYE which bears erect plumes of small snowy-white blossoms and green, pear shaped seed pods. These seeds, off the tree very poisonous, were used by Indians only after grinding and leaching very carefully.

LAUREL

Dense thickets of low growing CEONOTHUS are heavy with white and lavender-blue blooms in early season. Deer seek their green leaves for food and shade on warm days.

THE WESTERN AZALEA is strictly a streamside shrub, growing from two to seven feet tall. Its white blossoms contrast the dark green and brown forest nearby. Its love of water is evident as it leans far out over swirling waters with its beckoning plumes.

AZALEA

MANZANITA

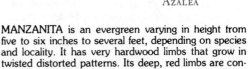

MANZANITA is an evergreen varying in height from five to six inches to several feet, depending on species and locality. It has very hardwood limbs that grow in twisted distorted patterns. Its deep, red limbs are contrasted by gray-green leaves, and white urn-shaped flowers. Its green and reddish berries resembling small apples (in Spanish manzanita means "little apple") were used by the pioneers to make jelly.

Gay QUAKING ASPEN are also water lovers and can be found in groves near streams between 6000 to 10,000 feet elevation. Their slim trunks grow to a height of 20-40 feet. The bark often indicates the scratch marks of passing bears and thoughtless humans. Their light green leaves, undercoated with silvery-white, flutter in the slightest breeze. In the autumn they present a great show in the high mountains when the graceful groups turn to gold, orange, and yellow masses of color.

QUAKING ASPEN

117

BACKCOUNTRY COMPANIONS

The forested slopes and lush meadows of the Sierra provide a great variety of shelter and food for many kinds of animals, large and small. Here the land, its coverage of trees, shrubs, and grass, and the moderate summer climate make up an ideal home for our woodland friends.

Traveling from the lower valleys to the barren slopes of the Sierra crest we find a continuous change in the kind and amount of vegetation. This makes a consequent change in the kind and amount of wildlife that lives in each elevation or "Life Zone".

The changing climate of the seasons too, affects their ways of life. To meet the demands of winter when food is scarce and temperatures may drop below zero, each woodland dweller must make special preparations if he is to survive. Most birds and some of the larger animals, such as deer, move down into the foothills below snowline where they find living more comfortable. This is called vertical migration.

Some animals can't or don't care to travel so far so they get through the long winter by sleeping most of the time and eating sparingly off their food caches. A few go into a deep sleep called hibernation.

Other animals, such as the chickaree and the cony, neither migrate nor hibernate. They have learned to make special nests in sheltered places and store up enough food to carry them through the winter. They hole-up during the worst storms. Then in good weather, they come out to scamper about and dig out the stockpiles of food they had gathered in the fall. To these hardy folk is reserved the privilege of seeing the Sierra's wonderland in one of its most beautiful moods under a mantle of glistening snow.

DEER

Because of its gentleness and graceful beauty, the California Mule Deer is seen and admired by more visitors than almost any other animal. After spending most of the winter in the foothills, the bucks migrate to the high country. The does, heavy with fawn, follow along and many of them make their residence in areas frequented by campers. This habit has developed, doubtless, due to protection they get from such natural enemies as coyotes, bob cats, and mountain lions.

The Mule deer is so named because of its large ears. In summer they are a reddish-brown but, with the coming of winter, this is replaced by the protective blue-gray coat.

Baby deer are called fawns and are usually born between the middle of June and the middle of August. Twins are quite common. Their inability to travel very fast or far when they are quite young is compensated by their mixed coloration or spots that makes them hard to see when they are lying down in the grass or brush. Also, they have no odor or scent at first, making it almost impossible for predatory animals to find them.

The bucks lose their antlers every year, usually along late in January or February. They begin growing a new set almost immediately. The new growth is covered with soft "velvet" that helps protect it until the antlers are mature. Along about September this covering is shed and they are very hard and sharp. When in the velvet the antlers are very tender and sensitive.

It is dangerous and very bad for the health of the deer to feed them camp scraps. They are naturally browsing animals and their food consists of tender shoots and twigs of brush, grass and when forage is short, even the tips of young branches. If they are given handouts around camps, they do not go out along the ridges and meadows in search of their natural foods. The old forget what they should be eating and the young never learn what is best for them.

Remember, we are visitors to their home here in the forest. This is their living room and we are their guests. Let's treat them with the kindness we would want if we were visiting the home of a friend. Deer are wild animals and, sometimes, are very dangerous. The bucks are cross when their antlers are growing and the mother deer will attack even children if they think their fawns are in danger.

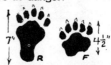

BEAR

All bears in the Sierra are called "Black Bear" regardless of their color. Some mothers have twins, or even triplets, all of different colors shading from black to cinnamon to blond. The cubs are born while the mother is in the deep winter sleep. They weigh from ½ to ¾ of a pound at birth, have no hair or teeth, and their eyes are closed for more than a month. They nurse for about six months and weigh around four pounds when they are old enough to leave their den. Mothers are affectionate yet strict in their training of the young. The first lessons include the climbing of trees to get away from possible enemies.

Although seldom seen in the wild, evidence of their activity is common in old logs torn apart where they have been looking for grubs, bear paths where each has stepped into the tracks of his predecessor, and bear trees. These latter evidences usually consist of claw-shredded bark, smooth areas where they have rubbed, and claw marks made up as high as they can reach—possible to advise others of their size and to "post" the area as their private domain. Their natural food includes berries, fruits, nuts, insects, fish, rodents, and, of course, honey when they can find a bee tree.

119

SQUIRRELS AND CHIPMUNKS
DAVID THOMSON

These are found in great numbers in all the forested areas of the Sierra. All but the chickaree hibernate in winter for 8 or 9 months. A few, such as the Golden-mantle and Belding ground squirrels and some chipmunks, are strictly terrestrial in habit. Their foods are mainly seeds, grasses, insects, fruits, berries, roots, and some meat when it is available.

Identification of each kind of animal is not difficult if a few general rules are followed. The chipmunks are the very small fellows and have stripes extending along the sides of their bodies on up across their necks to include the sides of the face. They also have very sharp pointed noses.

The Golden-mantle ground squirrel looks much like an oversized, well-fed chipmunk, for which he is often mistaken. His personality is as colorful as the yellow-gold or copperish mantle he wears. The black and white stripes on his sides do not extend to the face as on chipmunks. He is quite a panhandler and becomes very gentle around the camps.

The Sierra chickaree really gets around. His species is found in many parts of the United States and goes by the name of "red squirrel" in the East, "bummer" or "boomer" in the southern Appalachians, "pine squirrel" in the Rocky Mountains, and "chickaree" or "Douglas squirrel" on the West Coast. He is by habit arboreal—spending most of his life in the tree tops high above the ground and descending only to work over his store of cones or to travel to neighboring trees too far apart to permit his jumping across from branch to branch.

The chickaree is 12" to 14" long, is grayish brown on the upper parts and whitish tinged with buff on the underparts and has a black stripe on the sides separating the back and underpart colors. He has a very expressive tail and his vocabulary is remarkable with his call sounding much like "quero! quero!" When startled, or when his home area is invaded, this call is accelerated to a high pitched chatter that, for all the world, sounds like excited profanity. He is often called the "alarm clock of the woods" because of his noisy alertness.

Probably due to his untidy housekeeping and the desire to keep his enemies guessing as to his whereabouts, he usually has three or four nests in an area of some 500 to 700 feet in diameter he has "homesteaded" as his personal territory. So, it is easily understood why he is so busy, what with all his chasing of intruders, gathering food for himself and his family, and, all the while, being the "towncrier" of his township! He does not hibernate in winter. Even then, when most of the woods are abandoned or asleep, he is ever on the go tending to the affairs of his country. In the late fall he cuts huge quantities of cones and then stores them in hollow trees or under the edges of fallen logs. He usually cuts many more cones than he needs and it is fortunate that he does because all his neighbors, including the bears, sponge off of him.

In the High Sierra country near and above treeline there are several small animals that make interesting trail companions. In the open meadows is found the Belding ground squirrel, sometimes called the "picket-pin".

The marmot is the largest member of the squirrel family. He is 20 to 28 inches long when mature and has a heavy body with very short legs. His coat is a grizzled brown to blackish on the back, shading to a dull yellowish-brown on the underparts. He usually makes his home in a burrow near large granite boulders along the edge of the meadows.

The cony, or pika, is an Alpine member of the rabbit family. He looks like a small guinea pig with large, round ears. More often heard than seen, his plaintive "E E Chick! E E Chick!" cry has a ventriloquist quality that is most confusing when trying to locate him. Securing food is a simple matter as he eats the meadow grass and seeds nearest his home in the talus slopes. Since he does not hibernate in winter he spends most of his time in the late summer and fall cutting large quantities of grass and storing it in his hay-barns under the rocks. During the long winters, sometimes 8 to 10 months, he must live off this. Perhaps that is why he is so busy from daylight until dark when we see him in the summer. Even the one that is seen just sitting on a big rock is busy—he's watching out for enemies that might consider conies as good food—and his warning cry at your approach tells all the rest of them that danger might be approaching.

Other animals, seldom seen but often noted for their activities, are the Yellow-haired Porcupine that leaves his girdle marks on young fir trees; the red-brown Pine Marten that resembles a large weasel; and, the shy Coyote whose saucy yappings and doglike tracks along the morning trail advise us of his nightly wanderings.

Our feeling of security from injury by animals is assured as we review the records of the Park. Few cases of bodily harm are found except by deer and bear. There are evidences of where people have provoked the situation by pressing their attention where it was not wanted.

GRAY SQUIRREL

GOLDEN MANTLE GROUND SQUIRREL

SPARROW: (White-crowned Sparrow): Distinguished from other sparrows by black and white stripes on head with one white stripe running back above bill through center of crown. Light grayish-brown on back, underparts light. Seen near thickets in mountain meadows. Has melodious, plaintive song.

BLUEBIRD (Mountain Bluebird): Seen in flight on High Country meadows. Feeds on ground and spends considerable time perched atop a stone singing. Bright blue all over except for a lighter shade on underside. Female usually a paler hue than male.

CHICKADEE (Mountain Chickadee or Short-tailed Mountain Chickadee): His persistent, identifying call of "chick-a-dee" or plaintive "ee-chee-chee" is heard in the High Country. Found on the tiptop twig of tallest trees. Somewhat smaller than a sparrow. Top of head and throat dark; has white line over eye; cheeks and breast are also white.

JUNCO (Oregon, Thurber's, or Sierra Junco): Has quite dark "cape" over head and shoulders; underside is white. Light brown on shoulders and back, center tail feathers black, outer ones white, light-colored bill. Feeds on ground around base of trees. Seen in the High Country at treeline.

ROSY FINCH (Sierra Nevada Rosy Finch): Friendly companion of the high mountain climber. Seen in flocks feeding on snow fields or surface of a glacier. Nests in rocky cliffs along wind-swept ridges above tree line. Bright rosy hue on breast, rump, wings, and shoulders. About the size of a sparrow.

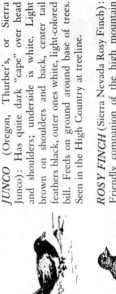

STELLER'S JAY: Large, flashy blue color. Noisy, raucous voice and bold, saucy habits. Lively companion in camp or along the trail. Large feathered crest on head that is dark extending to a blue-black on shoulders and wings. Light blue-gray on underparts. Larger than a robin.

WESTERN TANAGER: His flight in and out of sunlight and shadow is a thing of startling beauty. Often seen at the Mariposa Grove and on floor of Yosemite Valley. Vivid scarlet head, upper back and tail dark, wings black with yellow bars, rest of body a striking yellow. Movements slow and deliberate.

AMERICAN DIPPER (Water Ouzel): Perches on rocks in midstream, "posts" or bobs up and down when standing. Dives under water for food and propels himself with his wings when submerged. Nests at waterline or behind the spray of waterfalls. Slate-gray, shading to dark on wings and sides of head. Very stubby tail.

AUDUBON'S WARBLER: Has an unusually melodious song heard toward evening. Bluish-gray on underparts; yellow area on crown, throat, on sides near front edge of wings, and on rump. Smaller than a sparrow. Found in areas of oaks and conifers.

CLARK'S NUTCRACKER: (Clark Crow): Usually seen at tree line. Has a noisy cry, quite companionable to people. Pale gray body with dark wings, dark center on tail. Outer edge of tail feathers and rear of wings in white. Size and habits similar to Blue Jay.

RAINBOW (*Salmo gairdnerii*)

Labels: red · rose-colored band · dark green · small mouth · rose-colored cheeks · silvery sides tiny scales · rose-underside · red

Only trout native to Yosemite waters. Usually spawns in late spring and into midsummer in the high country when the fish work their way upstream into small rivulets.

BROWN (*Salmo trutta*)
(Sometimes called Loch Leven)

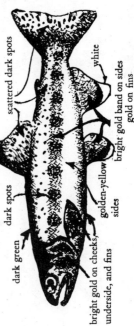

Labels: large dark spots (some black, some red) · brownish yellow · dark

Only trout in park with both red and black spots on its sides. Planting limited to large streams. Spawns in the fall.

EASTERN BROOK (*Salvelinus fontinalis*)

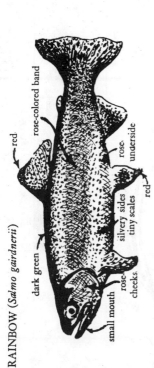

Labels: mottled olive and black blotches · red spots on sides · large mouth · reddish-orange fins margined in white

A heavy-bodied, large-mouthed trout. Common above 7,000 ft. Usually frequents deeper holes and slower-moving water than Rainbow. Spawns in the fall.

GOLDEN (*Salmo aqua-bonita*)

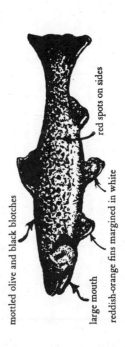

Labels: scattered dark spots · white · dark spots · dark green · bright gold band on sides · gold on fins · golden-yellow sides · bright gold on cheeks, underside, and fins

Aqua-bonita means "pretty waters." A native of Kern River country, especially Golden Trout Creek. Spawns in late spring.

IDENTIFYING THE MOST COMMON CONE-BEARING TREES

First examine the foliage and compare it with the sketches below in Chart A. Then refer to the groups in Chart B where the different conifers are listed according to number of needles in a sheath. Using this step as the base, observe the other physical characteristics, such as the general sil-houette of the tree, size of cone, texture and color of bark, etc. The eleven conifers listed below are arranged in a life zone sequence from the floor of Yosemite Valley to the timberline slopes above Vogelsang.

CHART A

GROUP I
Leaves in clusters. Tied with sheaths at bases

GROUP II
Leaves singly attached to branches.

GROUP III
Leaves appressed to branches.

CHART B

GROUP I
2-NEEDLE BUNDLES:
LODGEPOLE PINE
5-NEEDLE BUNDLES:
WHITEBARK PINE
SUGAR PINE
3-NEEDLE BUNDLES:
JEFFREY PINE
PONDEROSA PINE

GROUP II
NEEDLES ARRANGED IN ONE PLANE ON BRANCHES:
RED FIR
WHITE FIR
NEEDLES GROWING ALL AROUND BRANCHES:
MOUNTAIN HEMLOCK
DOUGLAS-FIR

GROUP III
ARRANGED IN OVERLAPPING SEQUENCE:
SIERRA JUNIPER
INCENSE-CEDAR

In using Charts A and B above it will be observed that most conifers having similar needle arrangements usually live most profusely in differ-ent life zone areas, thus simplifying the problem of identification.

NAME	SILHOUETTE	CONES	BARK	NEEDLES	RESIDENCE PREFERENCE
PONDEROSA PINE	100'-180' ht. 3'-5' dia. Trunk smooth, cylindrical, with little taper until crown branches. Limbs tip upward on ends.	2¾"-5¼" long. Oval shape, clustered near end of branches.	3"-4" thick. Surface divided into broad, shieldlike yellow plates. Surface broken into small, concave, flaky scales.	6"-11¼" long. 3 in a bundle. Deep yellow-green. Grouped in heavy, brushlike clusters at ends of branches.	3,000'-5,500' elevations. (Transition.) Very wide distribution. Most common conifer on floor of Yosemite Valley. Some approx. 8' in dia.
JEFFREY PINE	125'-175' ht. 1½'-4½' dia. Rounded top and many limbs. Large-bodied and straight.	5"-11" long. 3"-6" dia. Purplish cast.	1½"-3" thick. Reddish-brown, broken into deep plates by narrow furrows. Strong vanilla or pineapple odor.	7"-11" long. 3 in bundle. Blue-green coloring.	5,500'-8,500' elevation. (Canadian.) Some age up to 400 yrs. Becomes stunted in high, rocky areas. Seen at Glacier Point and Little Yosemite.

	Tree	Cone	Bark	Leaves	Elevation & Range
SUGAR PINE	 150'–200' ht. 5–8' dia. Flat-topped, long sweeping branches in upper third of tree.	 12"–23" long. 2½–5" dia. Pendent near outer ends of upper branches.	1½"–4" thick. Medium brown, deeply fissured segments tinged with red.	2½"–4" long. 5 in a bundle. Blue-green. 	4,000'–8,000' elevation. (Transition & Canadian.) North and east slopes of canyons. In Little Yosemite, Lost Valley, along Sunrise Creek, and on Glacier Point road.
INCENSE-CEDAR	 75'–120' ht. 2¼–4½' dia. Crown open and irregular on mature trees. Young have smooth, conical shape.	1"–1½" long. ½" dia. Urn-shaped when green. Sections roll back when ripe. 	3"–8" thick on mature trees. Cinnamon-red, deeply fissured with soft, stringy texture. On young trees is thin, scaly, reddish-brown, flakes off easily.	¼"–½" scalelike leaves covering twigs in tight, overlapping sequence. Very fragrant. Rich, shiny-green coloring 	3,000'–6,000' elevation. (Transition.) In Yosemite Valley some are 5'–6' dia. and 125'–150' ht. Those 2'–3' dia. approx. 300 yrs. A few reach 500 yrs. Lost Valley.
DOUGLAS-FIR	 100'–175' ht. 3½–5½' dia. Graceful, with long, sweeping branches.	 2'–4" long. 1"–2½" dia. Long, tapering, and pendent near tips.	1½"–3½" thick. Made up of thick, deep furrows. Brownish-gray on ridges. Sides of deep fissures are ash colored.	¾"–1½" long. Spiraled around branches. Needles, attached singly, are flat and glossy above and yellow-green beneath. Small branches have a plumy form. 	3,500'–6,500' elevation. (Transition.) Found on cool, north side of ridges. Long-lived; 3'–4' dia. are 150–200 yrs. while those 4'–8' dia. are 200–375 yrs. old.
WHITE FIR	 140'–180' ht. 3½'–6' dia. Very massive. Lower ⅓ clear.	3"–5" long. 1½"–2¾" dia. Erect on outer tips of limbs near top of trees. 	4"–6½" thick. Silvery on young trees. Ash-gray to deep brownish-yellow beneath. Young stems have resin blisters.	1"–3" long. Longest of any fir. Stands out from branch with a twist at its base. Green with whitish tinge. 	3,500'–8,000' elevation. (Transition into Canadian.) 3½'–5' dia. trees range from 275–450 yrs. old. Three unusual specimens along trail near upper end Merced Lake.
RED FIR	 125'–175' ht. 1½'–5' dia. Many with broken crowns.	5"–8" long. 2¾"–3½" dia. Stand erect near tips of branches. Purplish, edged with brown. 	2"–7" thick. Deeply fissured and divided by short, diagonal ridges. Outer scales dark red. Inner segments bright red. Surface rough.	¾"–1¼" long. Four-sided, rounded on top. Attached directly to stem. Limbs form heavy sprays in whorl formation. 	6,000'–9,000' elevation. (Canadian.) Trees 20"–30" dia. average 225–375 yrs. old. Found on Sunrise Trail, Snow Flat, and Glacier Point Road.
LODGEPOLE PINE	 30'–80' ht. 1"–2½' dia. Twisted trunks, often lightning scarred.	 1½"–2½" long. 1"–2" dia. Very numerous.	Very thin. Light gray and yellowish-brown. Very scaly.	1"–2½" long. 2 needles in a bundle. (Only 2-needle pine in Yosemite.) Yellowish-green, often twisted. 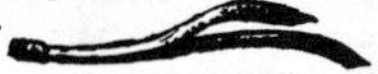	6,000'–10,000' elevation. (Canadian & Hudsonian.) Ages 100–175 yrs. common. Tuolumne Meadows and upper Merced River Canyon

MOUNTAIN HEMLOCK	 25′–100′ ht. 1′–3½′ dia. Limbs close to ground.	 1″–3″ long. ½″–1½″ dia. Abundant near top.	Young trees: thin and silvery. Mature trees: 1¼″ thick, reddish-brown, deeply ridged and furrowed.	½″–¾″ long. Grows spirally around branches. Appear thicker on upper side. 	7,700′ on up the cool, northern slopes to timberline. Trees 18″–20″ dia. and 50′–60′ ht. reach ages of 180–250 yrs. Upper Lyell Fork Canyon, east wall of Lewis Creek Canyon.
SIERRA JUNIPER	 10′–30′ ht. 3′–6′ dia. Heavy, twisted trunk.	 ¼″–½″ dia. Looks more like berry than a cone. Divided into three sections. Covered with whitish bloom. Very pungent odor.	2½″–5″ thick. Reddish-brown. Long, fibrous ridges of soft bark is easily stripped from trunk.	 ⅛″ long. Scalelike, overlapping in clusters of three, similar to incense-cedar. Gray-green.	6,500′–10,000′ elevation. (*Canadian & Hudsonian.*) On rocky hillsides. Older trees reach ages 500–1,500 yrs. High, rocky ridges near Merced Lake. Upper Lewis Creek Canyon.
WHITEBARK PINE	15′–40′ ht., 15″–30″ dia. in sheltered areas. On open ridges a sprawling, prostrate, shrublike growth. 	 1¼″–3½″ long. 1″–2″ dia. Oval-shape. Pitchy, thick scales. Purplish.	⅜″ thick at base to ¼″ on limbs. Dark gray on mature trunk blending to whitish on smooth, outer limbs.	1¼″–2¾″ long. 5 in bundle. Dark, yellow-green and thickly clustered near ends of branches. 	9,000′ to timberline. (*Hudsonian.*) 18″–20″ dia. are up to 300 yrs. old. 3½″–4″ dia. may be 250 yrs. old. Vogelsang, Evelyn Lake, Tioga Pass, Ireland Ridge.

High on the tip of rock-bound pine
Where the wandering winds are free,
Above sparkling brook and blue lake's shine,
Comes the plaintive song of a Chickadee.

Where Hemlock, Juniper, and Whitebark Pine,
With trunks so twisted and stark,
Mark life's vanguard at Timberline
Comes the Cony's cheerful bark.

EASTERN SIERRA PINES

The pines of the east and south slopes of the Sierra include three rather unique pines: limber, foxtail, and pinyon. They are not found normally on the west slope. High country visitors will find them in small, open groups scattered in between low ridges and even on open plateaus with little or no competition from other trees.

The *limber pine*, at maturity, reaches up to 50' - 60' with diameters up to 3' - 4'. Their thick, dark brown bark and long, spreading arms make a great photographic contrast against gray rocks and towering skylines. Its twisted, scraggly forms are seen all along the east Sierra slopes near timberline. Its limber quality is very flexible in withstanding severe storms. (Needles 1"-1¼" long in groups of 5. Cones 3½"-10" long.)

Refusing the sheltered life of low valleys and protected ridges, the *foxtail pine* in obstinate defiance seems to enjoy the high shoulders near windswept passes, high stormy plateaus, and shoulders of such inhospitable places as the 10-12,000' granite ridges along the Great Western Divide and Upper Kern Plateau. Standing erect they seem to challenge the elements and enjoy them at their worst. With diameter up to 3'-6' and heights of 60'-70', they attain ages of nearly 1,000 years. (Needles ¾"-1" long in groups of 5. Cones 2½" x 5" long.)

The *pinyon pine* occupied a special place in the life habits of the foothill and desert Indians. The profusion of large, oily, nuts from their cones ripening in the fall determined the coming and going of early peoples as they harvested the winter food. Pinyon nuts were a basic part of their "trade goods" with other tribes.

Groves, and in places, forests of pinyon pines present a rolling gray-green carpet over the dry east Sierra foothills and far east into the Great Basin Country. (Height 8'-25' diameter up to 12"-15". Cones to 3" almost round. Needles - only pine having single needle.)

Foxtail Pine at Lone Pine Lake   Rocky Rockwell, USFS

LIFE ZONE ADAPTATION IN THE YOSEMITE REGION

ELEVATION	TRANSITION To 6,200 ft.	CANADIAN To 8,000 ft.	HUDSONIAN To 10,500 ft.	ARCTIC ALPINE
PLANTS	Ponderosa Pine Pacific Dogwood Canyon Live Oak Douglasfir Bigleaf Maple Calif. Filbert Calif. Black Oak Greenleaf Manzanita Western Azalea Incense Cedar Bearmat Sugar Pine White Alder White Fir Calif. Laurel	Quaking Aspen Huckleberry Oak Rocky Mtn. Maple Pinemat Manzanita Jeffrey Pine Sierra Juniper Red Fir Bitter Cherry Mtn. Whitethorn Ceanothus Sierra Evergreenchinkapin (Sierra Chinquapin)	Whitebark Pine Mtn. Hemlock Lodgepole Pine Western White Pine Mertens Cassiope Brewer Mtn. Heath Bog Kalmia Gooseberry Currant Rock Fringe Sierra Gentian Wax Currant Dwarf Blueberry	Polemonium (Skypilot) Tufted Skyland Willow Least Lewisia Snowball Saxifrage Mt. Dana Hulsea Alpine Groundsel Alpine Mtn. Sorrel Alpine Buttercup Sierra Primrose Timberline Antennaria Lemmon Draba
BIRDS	Northern Violet-green Swallow Western White-throated Swift Calif. Yellow Warbler Red-shafted Flicker Calif. Woodpecker Sierra Nevada Red-breasted Brewer Blackbird Sap sucker Western Tanager Calif. Purple Finch Blue-fronted Jay Western Robin Western Wood Pewee Western Chipping Sparrow Western Warbling Vireo Dotted Canyon Wren Sierra Nevada Brown Creeper Western Belted Kingfisher Pacific Black-headed Grosbeak Northern White-headed Wood- Calaveras Warbler pecker Black-throated Gray Warbler Kern Red-winged Blackbird Pacific Band-tailed Pigeon Calif. Pigmy Owl Calif. Spotted Owl Saw-whet Owl Cassin Vireo Cooper Hawk	Western Golden-crowned Sierra Grouse Kinglet Hammond Flycatcher Townsend Solitaire American Dipper (Water Western Goshawk Ousel) Western Red-tailed Hawk Williamson Sapsucker Sierra Nevada Junco Yosemite Fox Sparrow Sierra Hermit Thrush Olive-sided Flycatcher Montane Lincoln Sparrow Western Evening Grosbeak Short-tailed Mtn. Chickadee Audubon Warbler Western Ruby-crowned Hermit Warbler Kinglet Cassin Purple Finch Red-breasted Nuthatch Pacific Nighthawk Calliope Hummingbird Green-tailed Towhee Western Tanager Great Gray Owl Mtn. Quail Pine Siskin	Mtn. Bluebird Mtn. White-Crowned Sparrow Clark Nutcracker Calif. Pine Grosbeak Sierra Crossbill Arctic Three-toed Woodpecker Golden Eagle	Sierra Nevada Rosy Finch
MAMMALS	Yosemite Pocket Gopher Boyle White-footed Mouse Long-eared Chipmunk Long-legged Bat Sierra Ground Squirrel Calif. Wildcat Calif. Gray Squirrel Calif. Mule Deer	Allen Jumping Mouse Yellow-haired Porcupine Sierra Golden-mantled Ground Squirrel White-tailed Jack Rabbit Bushy-tailed Wood Rat Yosemite Meadow Mouse Sierra Pocket Gopher Sierra Chickaree Tahoe Chipmunk Allen Chipmunk Sierra Mtn. Beaver Sierra Red Fox Sierra Black Bear Mtn. Coyote Mtn. Weasel Fisher	Belding Ground Squirrel Southern Sierra Marmot Sierra Least Weasel Sierra Pine Martin Southern Wolverine Calif. Badger Sierra Lemming Mouse	Yosemite Cony or Pika Alpine Chipmunk
REPTILES AMPHIBIANS	Rubber Snake Coral King Snake Sierra Nevada Salamander Pacific Tree Toad Sharp-tailed Snake Sierra Nevada Garter Snake Yosemite Skink	Tenaya Blue-bellied Lizard Mtn. Garter Snake Mtn. Lizard Sierra Alligator Lizard	Yosemite Toad Sierra Yellow-legged Frog	Mt. Lyell Salamander

EUGENE ROSE

Yosemite in Winter

Yosemite has become one of the West's most popular winter sports areas because of its ideal terrain, excellent recreation accommodations, and natural beauty. General activities include ice skating, skiing, as well as a ski school, and illustrated evening talks by Ranger Naturalists.

The facilities at Badger Pass include regular chair lifts and a beginner's lift. There is a large parking area, first aid, and a Ski House with a cafeteria, rental shop with modern equipment, and baby sitting provisions. Park Rangers provide reliable information and assistance.

The Yosemite Ski School was founded in 1928 and is connected with FWSIA. They have more than a score of full and part time instructors for group and private lessons, seven days a week. There are amateur competitions for all abilities and ages.

A daily bus service is available between Yosemite Valley and the ski area. There are no overnight accommodations or camping at Badger. There is no tobogganing in the ski area and no snowmobiling permitted anywhere in the Park. Most skiing is done on the packed slopes which are kept in good condition and supervised by ski patrols.

Other ski activities include seminars on survival, snow camping and ski mountaineering. Overnight trips arranged at the Mountain School. Ski-touring and Nordic Racing for beginners and family groups. For the advanced, a four-day ascent to Mt. Hoffman (10,850') or a trans-Sierra tour to the east side of the Park including Tuolumne Meadows and Tioga Pass.

The Park Service has provided a snow play area at Crane Flat where families can safely romp in the snow among the beautiful evergreens.

Inquire at the Park Ranger Headquarters regarding cross-country skiing on the Tioga Road. The road is closed to auto traffic in the winter but open to skiers and snowshoers.

Wilderness Permits, required for all overnight trips, are available at the Valley Visitor Center, Badger Pass Ranger Station and Hodgdon Meadow Ranger Station.

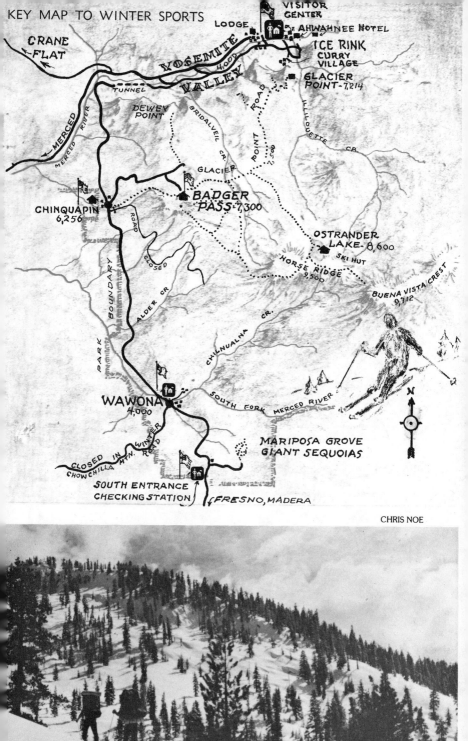

KEY MAP TO WINTER SPORTS

VISITOR CENTER

LODGE

AHWAHNEE HOTEL

CRANE FLAT

YOSEMITE VALLEY 4,000

ICE RINK

CURRY VILLAGE

GLACIER POINT - 7,214

TUNNEL

DEWEY POINT

MERCED RIVER

BRIDALVEIL CR.

POINT ROAD

ILLILOUETTE CR.

GLACIER

CHINQUAPIN 6,256

BADGER PASS - 7,300

OSTRANDER LAKE - 8,600

SKI HUT

ROAD CLOSED

ALDER CR.

HORSE RIDGE 9,500

BUENA VISTA CREST 9,712

PARK BOUNDARY

CHILNUALNA CR.

WAWONA 4,000

SOUTH FORK MERCED RIVER

N

CLOSED IN WINTER MTN. ROAD

CHOWCHILLA

MARIPOSA GROVE GIANT SEQUOIAS

SOUTH ENTRANCE CHECKING STATION

FRESNO, MADERA

CHRIS NOE

CONTOUR INTERVAL 80 FEET

SCALE 1:62500

UTM GRID AND 1953 MAGNETIC NORTH
DECLINATION AT CENTER OF SHEET

SKIERS AND SNOWSHOERS
PLEASE MAKE AND MAINTAIN
SEPARATE, PARALLEL TRAILS

MN
17°
302 MILS

GN
1°18'
23 MILS

0   MILES   1

132

BADGER PASS-GLACIER POINT ROAD

1. BRIDALVEIL LOOP (7 miles, 11.2 km; allow 7-8 hours)
   Starts at Badger Pass Ski Area, follows Old Glacier Point Road to Bridalveil Creek Campground, north to Peregoy Meadow. Return to Badger Pass via new highway to open roadend at Peregoy or Summit meadows.

2. △18 DEWEY POINT MEADOW TRAIL (3 miles, 4.8 km-one way; allow 3-6 hours)
   Starts at east end of Summit Meadow (7400'). Easy route along snow-blanket flats and forested slopes. Very popular, especially on weekends. Leads to south rim of Yosemite Valley west of Bridalveil Creek (7385'). Extensive view of lower end of Valley.

3. △14 DEWEY POINT ALTERNATE
   Parallels No. 18 but includes more difficult terrain and heavier forest cover. Allow one hour longer.

4. △19 GHOST FOREST LOOP (two routes)
   a. Begins at Bridalveil Creek Campground when road is open (5 miles, 8 km; allow 3-5 hours) b. From Summit Meadow allow 5-6 hours. This is a self-guided Nature Trail. Description of area is included in brochure available at Visitor Center.

5. △13 LIMIT TRAIL (3.4 miles, 5.4 km; allow 3-5 hours)
   Starts at Old Glacier Point Road, follows south to junction with Bridalveil Creek Campground Road and Merced Crest Trail (#16).

6. GLACIER POINT (7200') (10.5 miles, 16.8 km; allow 2-3 DAYS minimum)
   Starting at Summit Meadow this trip follows the Glacier Point Road all the way. Side trips to Sentinel Dome or Taft Point. Views include Illilouette Basin, Clark Range, Upper Merced River and Tenaya Creek Canyons.

7. △7 CHINQUAPIN SKI RUN (2.7 miles, 4.3 km)
   Trailhead just west of Ranger Station at Badger Pass. Follows down Old Glacier Point Road to Chinquapin (Hwy. 41). A fast, downhill run that drops 1700'.

BADGER PASS - OSTRANDER LAKE

Cross-country Ski Tours for experienced skiers only. Round trip is about twenty miles. Allow two full days minimum. Skiers should start out by 10 AM to ensure making it before dark.

8. △15 HORIZON RIDGE TRAIL (8.5 miles, 13.6 km)
   Trailhead is 4 miles east of Summit Meadow on Glacier Point Road. Look for Trail Marker △ where highway turns north to Glacier Point. This is the most favored route out to Ostrander Lake.

9. △16 MERCED CREST TRAIL (9.5 miles, 15.2 km)
   A long, strenuous route between Ostrander and Badger Pass Lodge. This trail is usually taken as a return route. Parallels the low, open, sometimes wind-swept Merced Crest. Danger of avalanches near Horse Ridge.

10. △19 BRIDALVEIL CREEK TRAIL (7.3 miles, 11.7 km)
    Trailhead 3 miles east of Summit Meadow, 1 mile beyond Bridalveil Creek Bridge on new Glacier Point Road. Route is a little longer than the Horizon Ridge route but doesn't require so much climbing.

11. △17 HORSE RIDGE TRAIL (2.5 miles, 4 km)
    Using Ostrander Ski Hut as an overnight base, it is a long day trip to the top of the ridge and back.

MARIPOSA GROVE OF GIANT SEQUOIAS

SKIERS AND SNOWSHOERS
PLEASE MAKE AND MAINTAIN
SEPARATE, PARALLEL TRAILS

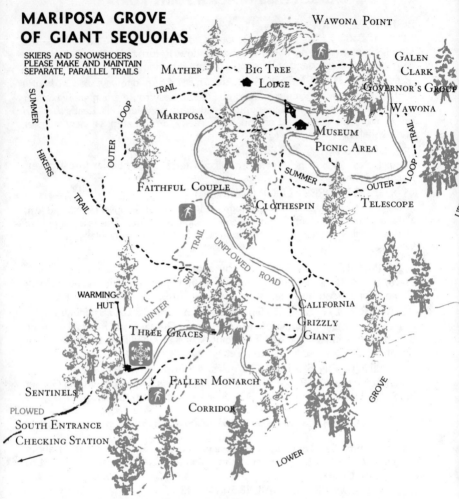

MARIPOSA GROVE WINTER TRAILS

The road up to Mariposa Grove is kept open as far as the Grizzly Giant. From there a ski trip of moderate difficulty can be made by following the road through the grove, including going out to Wawona Point. It is a rare treat indeed, to view these venerable giants following a heavy snow.

The Loop Road encircling the Grove provides an excellent route for skiers to visit most of the larger trees. Several short trails suggest a tour that follows the Loop Road all the way up to Wawona Point where the expansive South Fork Basin lies below. Then returning down the hill visit the trees in the Upper Grove near the Museum. (No overnighters here. It is only an Emergency shelter.) Continuing down past the Clothespin Tree, ski or snowshoe to the Lower Grove, which includes the Grizzly Giant and the famous Fallen Monarch. (Note: Toilet facilities only at the main parking lot and Big Trees Lodge in the Upper Grove.)

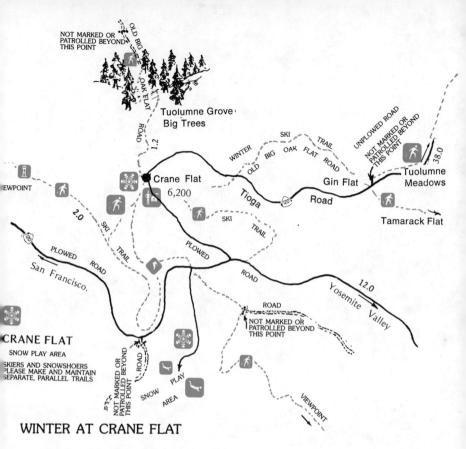

WINTER AT CRANE FLAT

This is a heavily forested area enclosing several long, open meadows. The Big Oak Flat Highway is kept open all winter and provides an opportunity at Crane Flat for a variety of snow activities, especially for family groups. Some of the winter fun and games are sledding, tobogganing, snowshoeing, and getting experience in overnight snow camping near a highway. The Tioga Road is unplowed beyond this point. The nearest food, gasoline and lodging are in Yosemite Valley.

Route ⚠ A Ski trail that follows the Old Big Oak Flat road from Crane Flat down to the Tuolumne Grove of Giant Sequoias. It is very steep and winding dropping down 500 feet in 1.5 miles. The magnificent trees are at their best when the dark green foliage and bright reddish bark is contrasted by snow-covered branches and neighboring underbrush.

Route ⚠ A two-mile trail is marked out to the Crane Flat Lookout. Views are most rewarding.

Route ⚠ follows the snow-packed Tioga Road 3 miles to Gin Flat. From there the old Stage Road leads to Tamarack Campground and Yosemite Valley. (This trail is not marked or patrolled beyond Gin Flat.)

Trails ⚠9 and ⚠10 lead out to a high shoulder providing excellent views across the Merced Canyon and on to the Clark Range.

East from Crane Flat the Tioga Road includes an extensive red fir and lodgepole forest for some twenty miles. Conducted 4-day trips are made via this route some 38 miles to Tuolumne Meadows.

Ralph Anderson, NPS, Yosemite

Your Security and Comfort

1. Stay on marked ski runs.
2. Don't start after 4:00 P.M. as darkness comes early.
3. Don't start runs or tours when bad weather threatens.
4. Accommodations are usually available only when arranged well in advance.
5. Some runs have good snow conditions only late in the season. Be sure to check on conditions before starting.
6. NEVER TRAVEL ALONE. Tell others where your party is going. Always check in with the Park Ranger before starting trips away from the road or Badger Pass ski center. Also, advise them of the approximate time you expect to return.
7. Do not take long trips unless there is an experienced leader in the group and you are in top physical condition.

MOUNTAINEERING IN YOSEMITE

Emulate the marmot, go climb a rock, or even a mountain to bask in the sun or to get a good view of what you came to enjoy. Fortunately, many of the best see-scapes are from places easy to reach. For example, some unforgettable views include: Sentinel Dome: a short hike from Glacier Point Road.

Wawona Point: At Mariposa Grove.

Old Inspiration Point: On the Old Stage Road above the tunnel.

Washburn Point Lookout: On the Glacier Point Road.

Olmstead Point: On the Tioga Road, just west of Tenaya Lake.

Lembert Dome: At Tuolumne Meadows.

The Cathedral Range: From Cathedral Pass or Vogelsang Peak.

Sierra Crest: From summit of Mt. Dana.

All of these require only average physical health, a short walk on an easy trail or, at the most, a few miles walking.

"Climbers" are a special breed who have an unusual outlook on travel in the mountains. They reverse the ethic of the pioneers who sought the easiest routes between two points. Climbers guides classify the peaks of the Sierra by a five point scale. Basically, Class 1 is a simple hike on a "walk-up" trail. Class 2 is off the trail and requires constant alertness selecting routes across boulder strewn slopes. Somewhat tiring to those with heavy packs. Class 3 involves the climber in risky situations. Can be somewhat unnerving to beginners. Class 4 are climbs with steep rock work, ropes, reasonably good skill and experience in rock climbing techniques. Class 5 is extremely hazardous—sub-divided into twelve categories of difficulty.

Most serious injuries in the mountains are from drowning, falling, or being struck by falling rock. There is a message in this. Man's greatest hazard is not from snakes, lions, or bear but from himself! Hiking accidents do not just happen—invariably they are caused by the injured person through inexperience, inattention, or poor judgement.

The following peaks of Yosemite and vicinity are generally classified as having routes of Class 3 or less in difficulty. Mountaineers and climbers' guides will supply more specific information as to approaches and difficulties. Eastern Sierra peaks often contain broad areas of metamorphic material that provide poor climbing conditions.

CLARK RANGE AREA

Grey Peak (11,574')	Mt. Clark (11,552')	Post Peak (10,996')
Red Peak (11,699')	Merced Peak (11,440')	Isberg Peak (11,009')
Ottoway Peak (11,440')	Triple Divide Peak (11,607')	Gale Peak (10,693')

CATHEDRAL RANGE AREA

Tenaya Peak (10,301')	Simmons Peak (12,053')
Columbia Finger (10,320')	Rafferty Peak (11,120')
Fletcher Peak (11,408')	(NOTE: Most of the Cathedral Range peaks are
Vogelsang Peak (11,516')	of Class 4-5 with many quite hazardous.)

SOUTHERN PARK AREA

Mt. Dana (13,053')	Mammoth Peak (12,117')	Electra Peak (12,442')
Mt. Gibbs (12,764')	Kuna Peak (12,960')	Rodgers Peak (12,978')
Mt. Lewis (12,296')	Koip Peak (12,979')	Mt. McClure (12,960')
Parker Peak (12,861')	Foerster Peak (12,058')	Mt. Lyell (13,114')

NORTHERN PARK AREA

North Peak (12,242')	Tuolumne Peak (10,845')	Regulation Peak (10,560')
Mt. Conness (12,590')	Mt. Hoffman (10,850')	Volunteer Peak (10,479')
Shepherd Crest (12,015')	Ragged Peak (10,912')	Dunderburg Peak (12,374')
Matterhorn Peak (12,264')	Cirque Mtn. (11,714')	Snow Peak (10,950')
Tower Peak (11,755')	Slide Mtn. (11,040')	Bigelow Peak (10,539')

CLOUDS REST FROM HALF DOME   CHRIS NOE

TRIP PLANNING

Yosemite's backcountry is usually open between the third week in June until the end of September. Actually, late season trips have fewer problems than early ones. The country is drier, stream crossings lower, mosquitoes are fewer, and snow packs are gone from most passes.

Most of the region is above 7000'. Days, usually warm enough to give serious sunburn, are followed by cold nights—many times frost on the meadow and ice in the water bucket. Select clothing and shelter accordingly.

Don't overexert yourself. The high elevations require some acclimation the first day or two. Estimate about two miles an hour on average trails—more crossing divides.

Be selective in what you include in your pack—take only what you REALLY need. Avoid canned goods and high water-content foods. Too much weight. There is plenty of water where you're going, consider only dried foods that keep well and can be cooked with a minimum of time and fuel.

Personal items should include waterproof container for matches, good pocket knife, ointment for sunburn or cracked lips, a few first-aid items, and a square of fine-mesh mosquito netting. Include up-dated USGS Topo maps and a compass. Keep yourself oriented. When you make rest stops relate what you see to what the maps show.

ON NOT GETTING LOST

Yosemite's backcountry trails follow along basins of the Merced and Tuolumne rivers. In addition to providing attractive routes they assist hikers in keeping well oriented as to where they are in relation to where they have been and where they are going. Keeping this in mind, backcountry travelers will find it difficult to get *lost*. Destinations are either *up* canyon or *down* canyon from where you *are*. If you do become confused, DON'T PANIC. Sit down and think about where you have been and where you want to go. If you don't know, STAY PUT. Someone will be looking for you if you filed a "flight plan" of your itinerary when you got your Wilderness Permit.

Rules and regulations of the Park are an outgrowth of what Rangers have found most practical in ensuring your well-being in the mountains and the need to protect the environment from the burdens of excessive overuse. Observe them, that you and others may come again to enjoy the wilderness.

When you are out there in the backcountry, minimize the impact of your presence by reducing the amount of wood consumed, erasing the evidences of human pollution and practice the PACK IT IN—PACK IT OUT ethic.

138

Yosemite Trails

With the first grey touch of morning light
The Traveler is roused from sleep
To follow the trail to mountain height
And view the grandeur at his feet.

From high on a shelf of the canyon wall
The Cliff Swallows dart and sway;
A Water Ouzel bobs at nearby waterfall
And the Canyon Wren greets the day.

Near mossy bank and Fern-edged rock
The Columbine waves its brilliant hue;
And the mind is cleared of care and talk
To drink in the depth of Larkspur's blue.

High on the tip of rock-bound pine
Where the wandering winds are free,
Above sparkling brook and blue lake's shine,
Comes the plaintive song of a Chickadee.

Where Hemlock, Juniper, and White bark Pine,
With trunks so twisted and stark,
Mark life's vanguard at Timberline
Comes the Cony's cheerful bark.

With the first star of evening above
The Bluebird, 'top a meadow stone,
Pours out his song of abiding love
To a mate nearby in grassy home.

Then winds in the treetops softly sigh
And the friendly eye of the camp-fire gleams;
With stars on watch in the Sierra sky
The Traveler is wrapped in woodland dreams.

Index

The materials for this guide represent a collection of knapsack and saddlebag notes gathered over the past five decades in Yosemite's High Sierra. Starting out as a guide, cook, and packer for the Curry Company, Mr. Clark became a fire guard, then Backcountry Ranger for the National Park Service at Yosemite. His usual assignment was patrolling at Merced Lake, Tuolumne Meadows and the North Country. His first guides to Yosemite's backcountry were printed more than twenty-five years ago.

As the years passed revisions and reprints have reflected the assistance and encouragement of many. Special thanks is given to: Leonard McKenzie, Chief Park Interpreter; Ron Mackie, Ranger, Backcountry Unit Manager; Henry Berrey, Business Manager, Yosemite Natural History Association; Mary Vocelka, Research Librarian, Yosemite National Park; "Butch" Jones, Backcountry Ranger, Minarets Ranger District, USFS.

FULL COLOR PHOTOGRAPH CREDITS
  Front: HALF-DOME – Richard F. Dempewolff
  Back: BRIDALVEIL FALLS – Ricahrd F. Dempewolff
  Inside Front: WINTER IN THE VALLEY – David Thomson
  Inside Back: MEMORIES OF THE BACKCOUNTRY
              Eugene Rose
IDENTIFICATION FOR AERIAL PHOTOGRAPH PAGES 12-13
Photo 182 U.S. Air Force – Courtesy U.S. Geological Survey

LEW & GINNY CLARK

Lew, a native son of a native daughter of California, grew up in Johannesburg when the Yellow Aster was stamping out gold ore daily. His father, Billy Clark was a teamster and operated the freight and stage route between Johannesburg and Skidoo. After acquiring his degree at Stanford, he taught history at all levels, from fourth grade to college. As a school administrator he worked in California, Idaho and Canada. His greatest joy was working as a backcountry Ranger in Yosemite and Grand Teton National Parks and as a Ranger Naturalist at Sequoia National Park and at Death Valley National Monument.

Ginny originally lived in New York State but immigrated to the golden west some thirty years ago. She was associated with such publishing firms as Harper & Row, Thomas Y. Crowell, Stanford University Press, and the San Francisco Chronicle. Being a mother of three kept her active before Western Trails Publications was established.

Together the Clarks have explored most of the fifty states, including Alaska, Canada, and Mexico. The guides they have written reflect a knowledge of the land and a concern about the care and conservation of our natural resources.

OTHER GUIDES BY LEW & GINNY CLARK

MAMMOTH-MONO COUNTY—THE guide to this favorite year round resort area. Includes Mammoth Lakes, June Lakes, Minarets Wilderness, Devils Postpile, Fish Valley, Crowley and Convict Lakes, and Rock Creek. Ghost towns and mining, history, geology and wildlife notes. 5 color maps, many photographs. $4.95

JOHN MUIR TRAIL COUNTRY—A profusely illustrated guide with many four-color maps, trail profiles, photographs of the Sierra Nevada between the lower Kern River Country on the south and the Emigrant Basin on the north. In great detail the Clarks describe trails to explore, lakes to fish, peaks to climb and what to see along the famous JOHN MUIR TRAIL. $5.95

HIGH MOUNTAINS & DEEP VALLEYS, The Gold Bonanza Days—The first book of its kind about the Basin and Range Country covering DEATH VALLEY, ghost towns, from Calico to Virginia City, Owens Valley, Ancient Bristlecone Pine Forest. With colorful maps, sketches, photographs, wildlife notes, services available, camping notes and travel conditions. $6.95

MT. WHITNEY TRAILS   Large folded 16" x 22" five-color TOPO MAPS includes Mt. Whit-
KINGS RIVER COUNTRY   ney and Sequoia National Park and the Kings Canyon National Park. Trail profile, up-to-date information and mountaineering notes. $1.50 each